"*A Prayer for Orion* is one of the most important books of our time. With heartbreaking honesty and wide-eyed clarity, James offers us an intimate view of the opioid crisis. Her vulnerability, compassion, and sagacious insight confront our tendency to judge or distance ourselves from addicts—and instead invite us to lean in and love."

Dorothy Littell Greco, author of *Making Marriage Beautiful*

"Addiction. Most of us don't know what we don't know. Katherine lets us learn with her on a journey of drugs and overdose with Sweetboy. A story filled with joy, fear, pain, deception, despair, hope, hope dashed, and hope restored. So many tears. And a God who comforts and sustains, who seems to disappear, then reappear. I wept, I held my breath, I turned the page—how can a mother endure? If you love a druggie or know someone who does, you will want to read this book."

Judy Douglass, director, Cru women's resources, author of *When You Love a Prodigal*

"With absolutely piercing prose, Katherine James shows us not only how to write but she also gently, vulnerably shows us how to pray, to trust, and to love even when walking through pain and suffering. I ate it up in two days! *A Prayer for Orion* is about more than a son's addiction or a mother's love—it is about the relentless love of God, who is present right through whatever we imagine as the very worst. Read it, let it move around your heart and propel you to love your people, your place, and your own Lost Boys."

Ashley Hales, author of *Finding Holy in the Suburbs* and host of the *Finding Holy* podcast

"Katherine James has done something most unusual. In her riveting memoir about her son's life-and-death battle with heroin, she captivates your heart and educates you at the same time. Every chapter left me eager for more. Spiritual, yet far from preachy, James created a powerful combination of raw authenticity with hope-filled truth. *A Prayer for Orion* promises to enlighten the reader while giving hope to weary parents who are walking a similar path."

Dena Yohe, author of *You Are Not Alone* and cofounder of Hope for Hurting Parents

"Baldly, bravely, beautifully told, *A Prayer for Orion* invites readers to see faith in its lived-in condition, how it can traffic in confusion as much as confidence. As Kate James understands from her son's story of addiction, to know God is not to be spared the grief of this broken world. It is, however, to watch hope—as small and inconspicuous as Elijah's cloud—grow heavier with rain. Inviting us to surrender every *what if?* for the settled peace of *even if*, this book is for everyone struggling to love someone well."

Jen Pollock Michel, author of *Surprised by Paradox*

"*A Prayer for Orion* is a memoir of sobering truth. James's incisive prose unflinchingly cuts to the core and reveals an incandescent, searing, heartbreaking-yet-tender story that will touch lives, especially those impacted by addiction. This book tells the truth, and in doing so it allows others to both hope and heal."
Alia Joy, author of *Glorious Weakness: Discovering God in All We Lack*

"*A Prayer for Orion* is more than the story of Sweetboy's battle with heroin addiction. Katherine James gives us a rare and raw glimpse of the way addiction traumatizes, distorts reality, and decimates individuals, families, and communities. There is a common phase in twelve-step groups: 'All addictions are cunning, baffling, powerful, and insidious.' Yet Katherine exquisitely and vulnerably shares how there is One who is wiser, more powerful, and persevering. . . . *A Prayer for Orion* is a must-read for those of us who are addicts or know one. It will remind us that we are deeply loved, we are not alone, and in Christ there always hope."
Sheila Wise Rowe, author of *Healing Racial Trauma: The Road to Resilience*, counselor and founder of The Rehoboth House

"I'd read the phone book if Katherine James wrote it. Thankfully, she chooses better topics, or do they choose her? Either way, *A Prayer for Orion* is one of the best books I've read in a long, long time. It reminded me of those familiar words by Frederick Buechner: 'Here is the world. Beautiful and terrible things will happen. Don't be afraid'. . . . Having read this book, I am more certain there is a light that darkness cannot overcome. *A Prayer for Orion* tells a terrifying tale, but tells it with such precision, elegance, and honesty, that it left me hopeful and unafraid."
Christie Purifoy, author of *Roots and Sky* and *Placemaker*

"Katherine James walks you into the intense reality of living with, caring for, and loving a person struggling with addiction and thankfully only flirting with death. An intimate look at what one should never have to go through as a parent. A poetic and cool narrative; a true perspective of a true experience."
Alexander Beh, author and filmmaker

"Katherine James's story in *A Prayer for Orion* reveals the universal cry in the hearts of countless mothers of addicts all around the world. This book will reignite the fight in you to stay in the war for your loved one's freedom! Katherine's message is crystal clear: Never. Give. Up."
Brian "Head" Welch, cofounder of the Grammy Award–winning band Korn, author of *With My Eyes Wide Open*

A PRAYER FOR ORION

A
*Son's
Addiction
and a
Mother's
Love*

KATHERINE
JAMES

An imprint of InterVarsity Press
Downers Grove, Illinois

InterVarsity Press
P.O. Box 1400, Downers Grove, IL 60515-1426
ivpress.com
email@ivpress.com

InterVarsity Press® is the book-publishing division of InterVarsity Christian Fellowship/USA®, a movement of students and faculty active on campus at hundreds of universities, colleges, and schools of nursing in the United States of America, and a member movement of the International Fellowship of Evangelical Students. For information about local and regional activities, visit intervarsity.org.

Cover design and image composite: David Fassett
Interior design: Daniel van Loon
Images: paper background: © Zakharova_Natalia / iStock / Getty Images Plus
star field at night: © Sarote Impheng / EyeEm
rust surface: © Prapass Pulsub / Moment Collection / Getty Images
stainless steel spoon: © Mubera Boskov / iStock / Getty Images Plus

ISBN 978-0-8308-4577-4 (print)
ISBN 978-0-8308-5792-0 (digital)

Printed in the United States of America ♾

InterVarsity Press is committed to ecological stewardship and to the conservation of natural resources in all our operations. This book was printed using sustainably sourced paper.

Library of Congress Cataloging-in-Publication Data
Names: James, Katherine, 1965- author.
Title: A prayer for Orion : a son's addiction and a mother's love /
*   Katherine James.*
Description: Downers Grove, IL : IVP Books, 2020. | Includes
*   bibliographical references.*
Identifiers: LCCN 2019041604 (print) | LCCN 2019041605 (ebook) | ISBN
*   9780830845774 (paperback) | ISBN 9780830857920 (ebook)*
Subjects: LCSH: Parent and child—Religious aspects—Christianity. | Drug
*   abuse—Religious aspects—Christianity. | James family.*
Classification: LCC BV4910.9 .J36 2020 (print) | LCC BV4910.9 (ebook) |
*   DDC 248.86293092—dc23*
LC record available at https://lccn.loc.gov/2019041604
LC ebook record available at https://lccn.loc.gov/2019041605

P 25 24 23 22 21 20 19 18 17 16 15 14 13 12 11 10 9 8 7 6 5 4 3 2 1

Y 37 36 35 34 33 32 31 30 29 28 27 26 25 24 23 22 21 20

For every lost boy and girl out there

He who made the Pleiades and Orion,
and turns deep darkness into the morning . . .
the Lord *is his name.*

Amos 5:8

CONTENTS

PART TWO

PREFACE

WILLIAM FAULKNER SAID that the past is never dead—that it's not even the past. He meant, of course, that our past isn't a benign thing—it's as much a part of us as the color of our eyes because in so many ways it has formed who we are now.

In writing this memoir I've had to discover and study the specifics of events and even emotions that I had no intention of going back to, but in doing so I've found Faulkner's words to be true; my past is not even my past. I am who I am because of it. It was a hard memoir to write, but there's no one else in the world who could write it.

My son has given me permission to write this. He's also said that I've probably gotten some things wrong, which no doubt I have, but he also agrees that my perspective is different than his perspective and that that's okay. I've done my best to talk with those involved in certain events to check for the accuracy of how things went down. I've also changed the names and descriptions of people to protect them.

PART
ONE

SICK

THEY SAY that when you tie a rubber tube around an upper arm, you feel the love the way a river feels a rock—a swish up or over or around. The river tightens and narrows, the wake behind it shoots out water like the universe shoots out stars, but the gritty fog of sediment tells the whole story.

The needle goes in. Rubber tube. Pull it tight. Flatten the arm. Needle.

YO

THIS IS THE WAY it happened, or at least the way Rick told me it happened. Sweetboy was nowhere around. I was in the kitchen. Waylen and Rick were in the breezeway sitting in the white Adirondack chairs. They're not the traditional Adirondack chairs—they're more square than rounded. There are four of them. Rick was sitting across from Waylen, who wore aviator sunglasses so you couldn't see his eyes, only yourself, and his curly, blond hair was pulled back in a ponytail. His thin and large knuckled hands were clasped in front of him. Rick told him that God wanted to help him and then they prayed together, and even though he couldn't see Waylen's eyes because of the sunglasses, when he looked back up Rick saw a tear run down Waylen's cheek. That's what he told me and that's what I remember, like I was sitting there with them—or to be more precise, I *was* Rick—looking at that tear, and behind Waylen was the yard and the different patterns of shade from the huge maple trees making their blue patches on the grass.

After that, every time I saw Waylen or talked to him I thought of the tear. As far as I was concerned it was on his face for good. Three years after that tear first appeared Waylen was dead of an overdose and his best friend, Stephan, was sitting next to his dead body in the hospital, never having seen anyone dead before, sitting there and praying because you never know, wasn't it about time for another Lazarus? And then Stephan was sitting there and watching Waylen's mother come through the door having just arrived and seeing her son and crumpling up, like her own body was finished with this life thing. Stephan took a picture of Waylen dead in the hospital and asked me if I wanted to see it. I said no. I wanted to remember the tear.

I know what it feels like to have your body crumple up like it's finished with this life thing. Like all of a sudden you realize that the only thing that had been keeping you alive was your son, and when you think he's gone your body tries so hard to die too, but it won't, so that's the most painful thing, that you can't get your own body to freaking die and you don't have any choice but to live. There's nothing you can do. He's dead and you want to be, but you're not.

* * *

Years ago I used to look at Orion's Belt through the enormous floor-to-ceiling bay window with individual glass panes in our living room and pray for our children: Sophie, Jules, and Sweetboy. The window leaks heat like breath through a cold fist, but I would stand there at night where I could see the stars and align Orion's Belt into one rectangular pane by shifting where I stood. I had a favorite pane that I liked to view them through, the second row from the top—when I stood just right, the stars went from lower left to upper right: Alnitak, Alnilam, Mintaka. Those are their names. Mintaka, that last star. Like the bitter end of a tightened belt.

* * *

It was in our living room with the bay window that I thought we might lose Sweetboy and called the police. Sophie, our oldest, had been married the previous month and Sweetboy had helped to string the lights and fix up the backyard—he'd looked so handsome in his suit with his crisp white shirt and auburn hair cut short and other than carrying a red energy drink around with him that ended up in all the photos, he'd looked like the perfect groomsman. Jules had flown in from San Francisco and sang Wreckless Eric's "Whole Wide World" at the reception.

Seven months earlier Sweetboy had told us he'd started doing hard drugs and wanted to stop so we'd begun testing him. He'd consistently tested negative so eventually we stopped testing him altogether. We were like parents at a PTA meeting sitting in back of the high school auditorium, nodding our heads in agreement while the principal lectures on about how bad the drug problem is, nodding because our own kid had done them and we knew how serious the problem was. But the truth was, although we couldn't know it yet, that one word, *had*, would be incorrect.

While the memory of those days has faded, the accompanying sensations have not. I think I would call the overarching sensation compassion, although I'm not sure that's quite right. I don't think we feel compassion for our children. What we feel is a paler, yet far fiercer, sort of mercy. It's meant for ourselves of course—this mercy, that without it will mean suffering the implosion of every organ within us—and we will go through any conceivable trouble, even giving our own lives, to achieve it. Even as I dialed, I didn't know where life would go because we might lose our son and then everything would change forever. I didn't feel angry, although it would have been appropriate—I lack in that department, which I've always assumed is at least one of the reasons I've lived most of my life with a dull, thumping bleakness that for some reason, in my visually inclined imagination, takes the form of a thick, fat hand pounding on an arterial door at the base of my neck. The door is probably made of horded muscle, formed over time from the mere act of staying shut.

I called the police because I found a text on Sweetboy's phone that stunned me. We assumed he wasn't doing drugs anymore. He couldn't be. It had been seven months since—at the encouragement of two of his friends—he had sat down with us and told us everything, told us we could test him. So we did. We assumed he was one of those kids who experiment with drugs, grow up a little bit, realize it's stupid, and quit. So many good things were happening. Kids' lives were changing. There was prayer. Our home was full of life. Although dread had accompanied many of my days over the last year, I was finally, hesitantly, beginning to relax. Initially, the last year had been full of the unique, solitary fear that only a parent of a child who's gotten involved with hard drugs can understand. Sweetboy had habitually come home at 4:00 a.m., sometimes not at all; he'd been smoking almost two packs of Marlboros a day. Once Rick found him snorting a pill, every phone call or trip out or text had been suspect. But the low, uneven sky had been slowly rising and Sweetboy, once again, was headed in the right direction. Things were good.

Our home had become a cross between a Billy Sunday revival tent and a carny—half church, half zoo—and while early on arms raised toward a canvas roof could just as well be seeking a high as redemption, the love of God was prevailing. Our home had become a gathering place for kids who wanted to hang out and talk. Rick had started two Bible studies. Tuesday evenings were for kids who were still using drugs, Wednesdays for kids who were clean and wanted to grow. Our living room was full of Sweetboy's friends, and friends of friends. Sometimes kids we'd never seen before. Our lights were on all night. The house was like a fishbowl, and with the cars bumper-to-bumper in our driveway and pulled up on the grass in front, and the bay window with the lit-up living room declaring all the people hanging out, I imagine there had to have been a bit of rubbernecking from the neighbors.

* * *

I saw the text around 11:00 in the morning. I had gone into his room to make sure he was awake, but I found him asleep on his back and covered by a blanket with one knee raised and his phone lying next to his pillow. He'd always tended to sleep that way, with one knee raised, which I could never understand because it implies some sort of tension while asleep, to keep your knee up like that. He was snoring. There was a slant of sun through the window that hit the wall as though it was about to ricochet and bounce quietly around the room, but it stayed in place, the golden light slicing the room in half. Sweetboy's skin is fair but he can still tan, and although when he was young it was a deep auburn, his hair is more of a brown now unless he's standing in the sun, where it looks almost red. Rick's grandparents were Irish and spoke in a thick brogue, and even though Sweetboy has the deep auburn hair and he doesn't always burn in the sun, there's still an Irishness about him, as though even though he doesn't have freckles, he should have them. His eyes are so dark you can't tell his pupils from his irises. I've never been able to tell them apart. Opiates cause the pupils to constrict into pin dots.

The language in the text was foreign; it wasn't the way Sweetboy talked, or texted. Or the way his friends talked, and at first I thought that he'd accidentally ended up with someone else's phone. *Yo, u want me to get u some* (I don't remember what he called it). *Ima go into the city tonight if u want some cheap. Gotta go the Dad's comin.* All I could think was that some greasy haired kid was in his basement with the TV on, texting everyone he knew so he could sell some smack (or whatever he called it). Maybe he had a bunch of baggies on a coffee table in front of him that he would spend an hour that night filling with some kind of powder he'd gotten after passing a wad of dirty bills through the window of some kind of dilapidated Chevy Impala or maybe a slick new Mercedes with the windows blacked out as it slowed to a stop and a guy wearing some kind of sweatshirt with some kind of hood up and half over his face would unroll the window. He'd be all pimply and pale because he didn't have a clue how to wash his face since both of his parents were addicts and didn't pay any attention to him growing up and he'd been hanging out on the street since he was ten. He wouldn't bother to look up at the kid who texted Sweetboy to see if he wanted some smack, or whatever he called it, he'd just take his money and maybe flip through the bills with his dirty unwashed hands before handing off the smack, or whatever he called it, to make sure there were enough bills before the Mercedes or dilapidated Impala slowly pulled away and turned the corner onto a dark street with a waste of syringes, like abandoned tampon applicators, clogging the gutters. I imagined dozens of Ziploc sandwich bags full of whatever it was the kid was buying—which I know now would have been enough dope to feed every addict in Philly for a month. I imagined half inflated CVS bags pressed into the grills of drains—heavy rains having tried, and failed, to pull them into the sewers. I know a lot more now, but back then I didn't have a clue.

✳ ✳ ✳

As I stood there with his phone, I felt a surge of both adrenaline and an antiserotonergic something take over. At that time I was trying to understand him at every angle; if I caught him in the midst of a turn or a glance, or with the light coming at him from behind, things would begin to make sense and fall into place; we could deal with whatever and tug him back into the earth's gravitational pull before some other space object grabbed his good senses and yanked him into oblivion. His iPhone was smudged and in a blue Otter case, which meant that it could survive getting tossed out a second-story window or thrown from a speeding car. My imagination had no end.

After seeing the *yo, ima, city* words on his phone, I brought it to Rick and silently handed it to him. He just stared at it. We both knew what it meant. I would say that the color drained from his face, although that isn't what really happened. I think his shoulders must have slumped a little, or his mouth opened a half-inch with no words; these are the sorts of things that make us say *the color drained from his face.* The phrase probably came about in an attempt to describe that visceral emptying that happens when you get bad news, news that changes the trajectory you were following before the bad news. I remember feeling like a little girl in the back seat of a moving car; the trees were going by, the fences, telephone wires doing their virtual jumps as we sped along. I could be all right as long as the landscape was on the other side of the window. The thick glass muffling everything—that's what it felt like, thick glass between me and The Bad News.

Rick handed me the phone and got up and went to the stairs and yelled for Sweetboy to come down. After fifteen minutes he still hadn't come so I went to the stairs and called again. "I'm *coming*," he yelled, slowly, like he was still pulling on his jeans.

He looked blanched and tired, a little confused, but also like he was beginning to respond to a terrified core somewhere within him. His eyes were sad, apologetic in their sadness. It was empathy I think, he had hurt us by hurting himself. Our love for him was never in question and he and Rick, in many ways, up until recently had been best friends. There was a heaviness in the room. His gray-looking face and his eyes becoming worried (or relieved? I wasn't sure) as the realization that we knew what he was doing dawned on him. Sin-guilt-sorrow-repeat. He had stepped over the edge and didn't know how to get back. Rick gestured toward the phone.

"Want to tell us about this?"

He shrugged, "What?"

"The text," I said. "It's from some drug dealer. I can't believe this . . ." I ran a hand through my hair. "I can't believe this," I repeated.

"Mhmm, yeah." There wouldn't be any stories. He knew we knew and was too intelligent to try to cover it up.

"How long have you been doing it?" Rick said.

"I don't know, three weeks, a month. I'll figure it out, you can test me every day."

"You need to go to a program," I said. It seemed like Rick hadn't quite caught up yet. The reality. He looked distracted.

"You have nothing. We're taking it all," I said. "No phone, no car, no computer. You need to go to a program." All I knew was that if you were addicted to drugs you went to rehab.

He tilted his head back and looked at the ceiling. "I need my phone."

"Nothing. No computer either."

"Just let me make some calls first. People need to know I won't have it."

"Not a chance."

He got up and went to his room. Rick went to the kitchen and I sat with the phone, turning it around in my hands. I prayed in whispers, tears flowing, and thumbed through his past texts, hating all the abbreviations like they were narcotics themselves: yo, aight, prolly, hbu: Percs, Vicodin, Mollies, Xanies.

He came out of his room, walking fast, went through the kitchen where Rick was standing next to the sink, and out the back door. When he left, Rick turned to me and held up a set of keys, indicating he'd taken the keys to his car, but they were the wrong keys; they were to our car. We heard the engine start and Sweetboy's Subaru peel out of the driveway.

* * *

I was afraid. Around 3:30 in the afternoon, I finally called the police.

* * *

You can't explain anything to the police when they have a protocol. I'm not sure if this is because of regulations set in place; some thick wad of spiral-ringed paper bound together in the eighties because of some situation that proved exemplary. Or, perhaps more likely, because people who join the constabulary are people who find it soothing to imagine that there's a thick black line down the middle of life that separates evil from good and every word they say, type, or refuse to say or type lies on one side or the other. When you've called the police and are in utter straights, anything you say that doesn't fit onto the blanks on the form that I assume they have on the computer screen in front of them is ignored. There must be a place for your words to be typed in so that they can drag the form into the folder that goes into the file before the PC quietly shifts into its dormant state.

I wish I didn't know what a 302 is. Did my son say something that would lead me to believe he was a harm to himself or others? I don't know. I don't think so. Before he left, with his hand on the doorknob, do I remember him turning around and saying, *By the way, I might hurt myself. I might hurt someone else?*

I've always been the kind of mother who packs the lunches with natural gummies and sandwiches made with non-emulsified peanut butter and whole wheat Ezekiel Bread. When they were in school I wrote notes reminding them of how much I loved them and how much God loved them. I slid the notes in with the food.

When I die I will—if given a proper amount of time before the tunnel, the light, and the Lord Jesus—look up one last time and smile to my offspring and my husband, and without saying anything, the smile will be such a perfect representation of peace that I won't *need* to say anything. My face will say it all. My children and my husband will linger for a while and then go back to their homes and try to occupy their grief with thoughts of seeing me again one day when it's finally their turn. I hope I've done that much for them. I hope that I've modeled how to, as the Bible says, *put your mind on things above.* The great Eternal Perspective. It chases us down, but in the end it's where you go for the peaceful smile so that the relatives can go home and sip tea and eat chicken salad and talk fondly about the way you stuck the notes in the lunches and bought the non-emulsified peanut butter.

As I tried to explain the situation to the dispatcher, I knew everything that was happening was real. But still, I held it all in front of me like a strange movie—someone else's movie—humming along in the middle distance, only it was important that I respond to the narrative, somehow insert myself into the story, because if I said just the right things and made just the right choices, it was still possible that my son would be healthy and young and vibrant, that Sweetboy would be back at his desk sketching racecars and making boats out of duct tape. It was still possible for things to be just like they would be if he had never tried heroin.

＊ ＊ ＊

I don't like to lie. That's why I didn't lie when I called in the 302 and the woman asked me if Sweetboy was a harm to himself or others. I knew that he was a harm to himself, and I told her so, but then I assume she paused with her fingers hovering over the keyboard, because then she asked me what he had *said* to make me *believe* that he was a harm to himself. He was not prone to outbursts or explosive emotion. I often wished that he would get angry or whine or slam the car door. I imagine there is some immediate drone of blood beneath his skin that's been fooling him into a state of languor for years, because I swear, if you were to take an icepick to the bottom of his feet, you wouldn't get more than a slight pulling away, like that unexpected jump the knee does when responding to the rubber mallet of a physician. The way I knew he was a harm to himself is because his full lips thinned the tiniest bit as he took the keys and went out the back door. He was pissed and scared as hell and I could practically smell the war inside of him. I tried to explain this.

"I know he's a harm to himself," I said with a shaky voice, and as-sumed the woman would acquiesce to my anxious state and quickly push the Big Red Button or the Large Emergency Lever that I imagined was within arm's reach of her office swivel chair. She would type in my son's name in bold caps, and this would immediately alert all officers in the area and neighboring states that Sweetboy was missing and in grave danger.

"What did he say to make you believe that he's a harm to himself?"

"I don't know, nothing. He didn't say anything. I just know he is."

"What did he *say* to make you believe this?"

"I don't know, he didn't say anything. *He just left.*" My voice trembled. I began to pace back and forth and kept looking out the window as though expecting every tax dollar we'd ever spent to show up on our lawn in the form of flashing lights, grief counselors, and helicopters.

There was a silence on the phone. "Look, for a 302 you need to have a reason to believe that he's a harm to himself or others."

To be fair, an officer did show up at the house, and he was very kind. When we opened the door he said, "There's a domestic here?"

"Oh, no. No," I said. "It's our son. He took the car and went into the city. To buy heroin." In my mind a "domestic" required me in a bad housecoat with a smoker's cough, yelling at my husband to get the crap out of my yard, etcetera, etcetera. . . . There would be a gun perhaps, or at least bruises, for evidence.

Rick put his hand on my shoulder and guided me back to the couch. He stood next to the door and talked with the cop. I put my head in my hands. I loved my husband so much right then.

"So if we see him, we'll stop him," the officer said as he was leaving. "We can't arrest him unless we find something in the car, but we'll definitely stop him." He shook Rick's hand. "Good luck to you both," he said, and Rick shut the door. Two hours later Sophie and Neil showed up. I hugged her and told her how much I loved her. I hugged her for a long time.

* * *

Sweetboy called later that night, around 1:00 a.m. I got a call from a number I didn't recognize. His words were slurred. "Hey, jus want you to know I'm a' ight."

"Where are you? Just tell me where you are."

"Nah, I jus' don't feel right about that . . ."

"Are you safe?"

"Yeah, I'm sssafe."

I sobbed. "I love you. I love you so much."

"Love you too."

THERE ONCE
WAS A MOTHER

WHEN SWEETBOY was born I felt the world split like my body split. Every cell in my body was so bloated with pain I imagined it radiating to trees and mountains, settling into meadows so far from me they were on another tilt of the earth—each jag of pain felt like lightning splitting my soul, as though every living thing was groaning along with me. He was ten pounds, nine ounces. Afterwards, when the cold set in with me shaking uncontrollably and my teeth chattering so much I couldn't even ask for another blanket and Rick with his back to me talking nonsense with the doctor who had done this so many times that I, over there on the table, was inconsequential, all I could think was how in the world had I just done this miraculous thing, getting a ten pound, nine ounce baby out of my body, and here no one seemed to care.

In the nursery of the maternity ward he looked like a gosling surrounded by ducklings. His face was rosy with life while the other babies had their little heads half turned to the side, fists pressed to their mouths. The nurses stood around him and stared.

"Vaginal birth."

"She didn't have a C-section."

"Not even an epidural."

I thought one of the nurses might poke him to make sure he was real. And I stared too. What if his cry was as big as his body? Head first, feet first, butt first, it doesn't matter: one baby coos and another one flips you the bird.

But I would rather experience the pain of Sweetboy's birth a thousand times over than relive the pain that I would have to endure years later as I saw his face grow pale and gray and then blue, when the oxygen wasn't getting to his brain. Emotional pain is far worse than physical pain. After all, it's the emotional pain that leads to suicide. I think this is because emotional pain has the potential to be infinite. Physical pain has to stop sometime. The bodies in the earth, all closed up in their caskets, they're not wailing because their legs hurt or they ache with fever. If they're wailing at all, it's the emotional pain of it. The loneliness. The boy or girl or husband or friend they thought they would have forever, gone and that's that.

We're all stunned by the evil in the world. Although The Evil is why so many people reason that God doesn't exist, I think it's proof that he does; if bad exists then good exists. I think for the sake of character development of personified things, throughout this book I'll call bad The Evil, and good I'll call God. The earth is a battleground. If I was a swearing girl, here is where I'd say, *Shit, the bullets are buzzing past our ears, can't you fucking hear them?*

There is good and there is evil. But here I'll contradict myself and remind you to think critically as you read my reflections. In short, it's complicated. And if good and evil were represented by a right and a left hand, the two would be as intertwined as that childhood rhyme: *here is the church* (two hands locked together, knuckles up), *here is the steeple* (index fingers rise together above the hand to form a steeple), *open the church* (flip hands over and open palms), *and see all the people* (intertwined fingers wiggle like so many congregants).

✳ ✳ ✳

The next morning, the morning after Sweetboy left, and after he'd called me in the middle of the night to let me know he was okay, Sophie, her new husband, Neil, Rick, and I sat in the living room opposite the bay window in front of our large stone fireplace drinking coffee. Even though many nights I'd looked through the window at the stars and prayed for our children, the panes felt hollow to me now, like they'd betrayed me and there was nothing beyond them after all and I'd misunderstood those moments and had only been staring out at the agony of life, the distant flames of what in truth were dying stars. As we talked, I was having trouble concentrating. I kept thinking about Sweetboy's phone call the night before, that he'd called to reassure me that he was okay. The boy who called me was the boy I knew: intuitive, wise, thoughtful Sweetboy. Since then his intuition had morphed into judgment and the motivations of others were always suspect. We were mid-conversation when Sweetboy's friend Jeremiah called. I set down my coffee and picked up my phone.

* * *

In 2 Corinthians, St. Paul writes, "I know a man in Christ who fourteen years ago was caught up to the third heaven—whether in the body or out of the body I do not know. . . ." Paul more than likely is referring to himself here, probably because the experience was too powerful, or wonderful, or indescribable, to write about in first person. And in his gospel, the apostle John refers to himself as "the disciple whom Jesus loved." Some things are too astonishing to imagine ourselves a part of, so we can only describe them at arm's length. And just as the goodness and wonder and outrageous reality of the third heaven must have been indescribable, so there are some things that are too evil, or too heartbreaking, to describe. So we keep them at arm's length. We become the furniture in the room instead of the human in the room, and disassociate.

There once was a mother who had a son. She loved him very much.

* * *

"Hey, we can't wake Sweetboy up," Jeremiah said, when the mother picked up her phone. He sounded confused, like he was talking to someone else at the same time, like there might have been a group of people with him, circling something or someone, like they didn't know what to do about a strange thing they were all looking at.

The mother stood up. Her husband and her daughter stopped talking and looked at her.

Jeremiah said, "He's breathing, but he's really blue and he won't wake up."

"What?" the mother's voice caught and she ran a hand through her hair. She looked at her husband.

"He's blue. I mean he's breathing, but he won't wake up."

"Call 911!" she yelled, "Now!" The husband stood up too. The mother bent forward, a hand on one knee. The daughter took the phone away from her and started talking to Jeremiah.

✳ ✳ ✳

It's sunny and warm—no, hot. The daughter gets the keys to her parents' car and tells her mom and dad to get in. The mother gets in the back and the father gets in the front. The daughter speeds across town. They get stuck in traffic and the mother can't seem to breathe. She's taking in air too fast or too slow and she's forgotten how to breathe. In, out, but how much? It's such a difficult thing to under-stand, breathing. How did she ever learn to do it? Her hands shake and she tries to call someone and ask them to pray. The numbers on her phone are too small and she hits the wrong ones. It's possible that what's happening isn't real . . . her blood is turning to water, or wax, her mind is an engine trying to catch. The mechanic would say it's failing to turn over. Is this her fault? Something went wrong . . . The man in the front seat, her husband, prays out loud, *Please, oh Lord, we need you.* He says, *Please let Sweetboy be okay. Please.* The mother says, *Please God. Please.* The daughter isn't praying because she's trying to get around the traffic.

Everything is sharp because it's too bright and it hurts her eyes. There is a long driveway that might be gravel but it's too dark to be gravel, so it must not be, and an ambulance with the back doors open. Everything is so bright that it hurts. There are reflections. There are trails of light; heavy imprints of color, residue from things that move. The ambulance doors. The large blue garage. There is a grass hill that her knees have to walk up, and then through a gate there is a pool. The pool is far too luminous to look at. It's made of light and is translucent in the periphery of the mother's eyes. There are sliding glass doors, a pool house, a group of kids. There is a small tree with some shade. People are yelling from inside the pool house—questions: "What did he take?" She sees a boy with long dark hair wipe away a tear. Louder, "What did he take?" The mother understands this to mean that whatever they are doing to revive her son isn't working. There is a loud, heavy slowness to everything: the voices, the movements. Did her husband leave? She doesn't see him. Where is he? This is her fault. Where's her daughter? They have to fix it. Whose fault is this? There he is, her husband. They tell him he can't go inside the pool house. They're working on him. Stay out here.

The mother is under the tree with the little bit of shade and she gives in to the waxy-water blood and slumps to her knees. There is another mother with blonde hair and very blue eyes, as light as the pool. She stands next to her. A large woman wearing a dark blue shirt that says EMT in white letters is backing out of the sliding glass doors. She is guiding a bright yellow or orange gurney, something that's neon and collapsible. It has bars and levers and warning stickers on it. Orange bars crisscross and fold and flatten and pop up. The wheels have padded brakes and there is a thin pad, blue, half hidden by a white draped sheet. The large woman in the dark blue shirt that says EMT pulls and guides the gurney, working at getting it over the threshold of the pool house. There is another EMT, a man, at the other end of the gurney. He is pushing it. He is leaning over the stretcher, readjusting an oxygen mask and holding something plastic even as he pushes. The blonde woman who is a mother too comes to her and stands in front of her so she can't see the bright orange gurney that pops up and down. She puts her hands on the mother's shoulders and looks her in the eye. *I just want to warn you,* she says. *He is very blue.* These are the words she says to the mother. She doesn't want to see her blue son so she turns away, and her knees are gelatinous and there is no bone so she sinks her body all the way into the grass.

I'm kneeling on the grass and pressing my hands fiercely over my face as though I can push my life backwards, as though I can choose now not to meet Rick in college, not to have Sophie, or Jules, or Sweetboy, as though there's something I can do that will transubstantiate the moment into a painless one, something innocuous and without meaning. As though if I had never loved anyone The Evil would have no interest in me.

We follow the ambulance to the hospital and watch as they push our son through the heavy glass doors. It's July 1st.

WAR DRUG

IT'S APPROPRIATE that heroin began as a war drug. Originally it was called by the less beastly name, morphine. In the 1950s my grandfather was a pharmacist in Deming, New Mexico, a town where cowboys were commonplace; my mother says she didn't think anything of the fellows who would come into the store all dirty and looking hopeless, even in their boots and cowboy hats. My grandfather used to fill prescriptions for their cattle and horses, then they'd go outside, walk around to the back of the store, and take it themselves. They didn't care as much about the pain of their livestock as they did their own pain sans opiate. I can only imagine the amount of morphine it would take to quiet a cow.

He owned one of the first Rexall Drug stores and after school, while my grandmother was busy at the Women's Society for Christian Service, my mother would head over to the store. She'd pull open the heavy glass door, smooth down her dress so it wouldn't get caught when it closed, and lie on the floor next to the magazine rack, belly on the linoleum, and read Wonder Woman and Donald Duck and Superman and Mickey Mouse comic books. On the other side of the store was a soda fountain but she wasn't allowed to eat before supper so she didn't go there. I imagine she must have known every shelf and candy bar in the store. She told me a few times she was allowed to bring her friends there for supper and they ate tuna salad and chicken salad sandwiches with ice cream sodas and milkshakes. The addicted cowboys would gather at the pharmacy counter, thin and frail, and wait for their prescriptions. No one considered them dangerous, just hopeless. They looked sick. When she asked my grandfather about them he said they had a disease.

I visited Deming when I was around eleven. There's a picture of me sitting on a curb in front of our motel. My skin wasn't used to the bleached sky, the sun invisible within its own chalky pale, which covered my face with freckles and turned my hair red. In southern New Mexico the sun doesn't skim things, it sinks in and transfers itself until mud turns to bricks and the dust skates over flat roads of heat.

My grandfather told my mom people sometimes just let the addicts shoot themselves because they knew there was nothing anyone could do to help them. He told her he was amazed at the way their thighs were riddled with needle marks, which I guess meant they were in the habit of using the top of their legs to shoot up, although that doesn't make sense to me because it would be awfully hard to find a vein in a thigh. Maybe it was actually their ankles. One time my mother asked her father how many times you had to take a drug to be an addict and he held up one finger. He said they probably got addicted during World War II.

There was a lot of cluelessness regarding painkillers during the Second World War. The general idea was that their addictive qualities were a problem to be dealt with later, after the important stuff was out of the way, like making atomic bombs. The first bomb was exploded one hundred miles away from Deming in the White Sands Proving Grounds. I imagine it exploding in the desert so powerfully that it bounced half the sun back at itself, but in reality, it happened at night. The explosion woke a lot of people up, including my mother, and the men who had stared at it through military grade dark glasses told the press that an ammunition dump had exploded. Never mind the addicts shooting themselves; in the end the bomb ended up killing a lot more people. I imagine infinitesimal carcinogens becoming entangled in organs and veins, ready to make their cancerous appearance some startling day years from then. A call after tests, a silent pause on the line as some woman who had dutifully attended the Women's Society for Christian Service or man who'd stared through military grade binoculars heard they had cancer of the pancreas or ovaries. When the atom bomb went off in the middle of the night, even though they were told otherwise, everyone knew the explosion was some kind of secret weapon. My mother imagined a ray gun.

Soldiers who came home from WWII addicted to opiates were said to have Soldier's Disease and before that, in the Civil War, morphine was the only pain medicine available for when a man needed a leg sawn off; they weren't always left on a table with only a swig of whisky and a stick to bite on in the way I've always imagined. Museums and movies make much of the rawness of it, the unbearable pain they had to live through. We put our hands over our mouths as we watch movies with soldiers covered in blood on stretchers in canvas tents getting legs or arms sawed off like firewood and wonder how in the world they ever did it.

But of course, even after the leg was long gone, they still wanted the morphine. Eventually, so many soldiers ended up with Soldier's Disease that Bayer Pharmaceuticals began pushing a new drug they claimed treated the disease. They'd figured out a way to boil down morphine into a different drug that they said took away the desire for the morphine, which was true—it completely eliminated the soldier's desire for it. Bayer called the new drug heroin.

These days we are very unlikely to have our legs sawn off. But there's a decent possibility we'll get our wisdom teeth removed, or twist an ankle, which in America is reason enough to go home with a bottle of opioid painkillers.

It's easy to blame the tendency of dentists and physicians to over-prescribe for America's opiate crisis, but it's important to understand that up until recently doctors were taught in medical school that one of their primary responsibilities was to relieve a patient's pain. In the 1990s OxyContin had just come on the market and its manufacturer, Purdue Pharmaceuticals, aggressively pushed it as an opioid pain reliever that, in light of its extended release properties, wouldn't lead to addiction. A safe opioid medication. Finally, physicians could do even better than "do no harm"—they could make everything pretty awesome.

But Purdue Pharma was wrong. OxyContin is addictive—turns out it's even more addictive than morphine—and the company has since had to pay $600 million in fines and damages for misbranding its product.

There have been many unsuccessful attempts to create a nonaddictive opioid pain reliever. In the 1970s Knoll Pharmaceuticals added acetaminophen to hydrocodone and called it Vicodin, the theory being that since high quantities of acetaminophen can cause liver damage, people will be careful not to take too much. But addicts are a tenacious bunch, and some innovative soul has figured out a way to separate the opiate from the acetaminophen. It's called cold water extraction and it involves coffee filters and freezers, and unfortunately, it works.

* * *

Graphs confirm the existence of a problem. Charts prove legitimacy because unless we can see with our eyes and follow a red line with our finger, how do we even know what's happening five states over? Overdoses are nothing but rumors until we see a chart. But it is in fact true: Illinois, Massachusetts, Georgia, the opiate epidemic extends across America. It's aggressive and predatory, and the numbers of overdoses are climbing. The charts all look the same; the line on the graph often hovers somewhere around zero. Bottom left, it begins its climb, mild at first, but then there's a pretty decent slant up before the opiates-are-the-most-awesome-manufactured-things-in-the-world year of 2011, at which point the line shoots up almost perpendicular, like some kind of fueled rocket. That's when we bow our heads and start to pray.

In America there were more than 64,000 deaths from overdoses in 2016. Overdoses increased 30 percent between 2016 and 2017. In large cities the number is higher at 54 percent—and higher still in the Midwest at 70 percent.

Since 2000 there has been a 200 percent surge in overdoses in America. In Philadelphia—where Sweetboy drove that afternoon in his Subaru—there were nine hundred fatal overdoses in 2016 alone.

One hundred fifteen people die every day from opiate related overdoses.

Every 18 minutes someone's on a floor, or in a car, or on a sidewalk, turning blue.

Gray Death is a term that refers to heroin that's been cut with whatever the dealer has on hand. Adderall? Ecstasy? With a name like Gray Death you'd think folks would steer clear. As per its name, it's gray, darker than heroin, and clumped together like some kind of tiny cuticle sized moon rock. If I found it on my back patio I'd probably toss it in the garden like a stray pebble. The next morning the Black-Eyed Susans would be half dead, their dark irises shrunk to telltale pin dots in the sun and their leaves wilted to paper ennui.

These days heroin is frequently cut with fentanyl. Fentanyl has elbowed its way into the opiate conversation and killed a lot of unsuspecting, ignorant, or desperate people in the process. It's a synthetic opioid, usually given to patients with cancer, and is 50 to 100 times stronger than heroin. It only takes enough to sprinkle a thin, tiny white beard on Lincoln's copper penny face to be fatal. But there's also something even more toxic that few know about: carfentanil, a true monster. It's one hundred times the strength of fentanyl. A couple white grains sprinkled on one of Lincoln's pupils can easily send someone to the morgue. A crocodile could fit down its esophagus.

* * *

A lot of people live like they're going to die, which must be a necessary way of thinking for a heroin addict. There's no way for them to tighten up the hatches and wait for the storm to pass; they're continually compelled to step into the storm and risk their lives.

Unconscionable because of repeated practice, dealers will sometimes slip a little too much fentanyl into a bag or two of their latest batch of heroin before it hits the streets. Their intent being to cause one or two overdoses because overdoses show that the product is good—that as long as you don't overdose on it, it will give you a great high. This is how a dealer gets a good reputation, by killing a few for the purpose of proving his product isn't weak, that it's not cut with baking soda.

One dealer said it was a necessary sacrifice. He shrugged and said, "Sure I feel guilty, but sometimes you have to sacrifice someone. It's just the way things are out here."

THE SALVATION OF MENSTRUAL CRAMPS

WHEN RICK and I started dating it was winter, and all the students were protesting apartheid: we signed petitions, there were marches, we boycotted classes, and there were sit ins. There were rallies and there was solidarity and there was Hacky Sack. One afternoon I was in a figure drawing class standing at my easel and sweating next to a radiator because the classes were always too hot. I went to one of the windows and propped it up with a stretcher stick to let some cool air in. There were two green tents weighted with snow still set up on the quad, remnants of the latest protest. I saw a kid with long blond dreads wearing baggy fatigues ride down a shoveled sidewalk on a motorized skateboard—I'd seen him before, usually with a girl in fatigues too, long blonde hair, stringy, but not in dreadlocks, and she'd always seemed telegenic to me, as though she should be featured in a documentary. The cooler air felt nice, but when I went back to my easel to finish my charcoal drawing, I saw goose bumps on the model's arms so I went back to the window, pulled out the stick, and closed it. The next day the tents were gone. Reagan was president then and Dylan was in his Jewish phase. Every once and a while B. B. King came to a small theater in town. I saw Dylan once and B. B. King twice.

During my sophomore year I started going to a Christian fellowship at Hendricks Chapel, a large, domed church in the middle of campus. The first time I went was because of menstrual cramps.

A week earlier, as they did every month, my insides had raged like pea gravel was drubbing my uterus. I had endometriosis and sometimes the pain was so bad I threw up—one time my roommate called an ambulance because she thought I was throwing up bile. I vaguely remember her saying that to the EMTs, that I was throwing up bile. Without fail, every month I would curl up in a ball and beg God to take the pain away. When I felt better I'd get up, get dressed, and go out into the world healed for four weeks until the next one. After the pain was gone it was peace like a river; all was good again, the world and everything in it, never mind that the pain was destined to eventually return. Unless I was folded over in pain begging for relief, I didn't think much about God.

During Sukkot, the Jewish kids who wore yarmulkes built booths made out of sticks and evergreen branches next to Hendricks Chapel and it fascinated me. I wasn't sure why they built them or who their God was—the whole thing seemed like a mystery that I knew I could figure out if I put in the effort, but I never really bothered to try. I also wondered what the Jewish kids did during Hanukkah other than light candles; I imagined them sitting around oval tables in dining rooms with menorahs on buffets praying and eating slices of eggs. I once watched a show on TV about an orthodox Jewish girl who was in love with her guitar teacher. She would leave her house, secretly put on a leather vest and a little makeup and walk into town with her guitar hung over her shoulder to see him. He was older than her and he knew she had a crush on him, so he finally sat with her on park bench and explained why he couldn't date her. It was an after school special so there had to be a moral to it, maybe that you shouldn't date older guys, but it only made me want to date an older guy because the guitar teacher was adorable and played quiet folk songs. After he told her he couldn't date her she went back home, changed, took her makeup off, lit the candles for dinner, and recited a prayer in Hebrew.

One Saturday night my roommates were getting ready to go out and one of them, Hope, kept trying on outfits and asking us what she should wear. I loved her voice because it was soft and raspy like she'd just woken up and had her arms out, stretching them like the actors do in Tylenol PM commercials. I wondered if she might have talked her raspy voice into existence, like she'd spent every moment of her life talking and it was beginning to dry up.

She was pulling up a black skirt and said she didn't have any clean underwear. I was sitting in a beanbag chair on the other side of the room.

Lauren, my other roommate, stood back and said, "The collar of your shirt looks like fangs."

Lauren tried to straighten the collar. "It doesn't look right, it's too long. And pointy."

"I don't have any clean underwear," Hope said again.

"So buy new ones."

"I already did. I went through those too." Cute foggy laugh, "I'll start turning them inside out," cute foggy laugh. When they left, she was wearing the skirt and a pink sweatshirt with the collar ripped off like Jennifer Beals's in *Flashdance*.

"Have a good time," I said.

* * *

After Lauren and Hope left, my cramps started—mild at first then the tightness increasing until the familiar waves of pain began and I started whispering my mantra again, begging God to make them go away and telling him I was sorry for drinking too much and if he'd only heal me I'd stop. But this time, like a kind of spiritual hiccup, it occurred to me that the God I was begging might not even exist, and I suddenly felt a massive, heavy glob of some sort roll over on top of me and begin to erase every prayer I'd ever prayed. It suddenly occurred to me that if God didn't exist, then I was free; without God, people could do whatever they wanted, and like little Sputniks flying around on the verge of expiring we could orbit anything—and even though I'd have to give up on prayer, I couldn't help thinking that maybe my life would be easier if God didn't exist. It wouldn't matter whether I drank, or missed class, or never went to church again.

But then, as fast as the thought appealed to me, it terrified me. That glob, or orb, or Sputnik that looked like freedom and could erase every prayer I'd ever prayed, would also make my life meaningless—God *had* to be real, I needed God to be real. It was one big either/or, and without him my cramps might never go away and I'd die in an airplane crash or a stampede at a concert, and all I'd see right before the world went blank would be the sweep of lit jet fuel through a cabin or the up-close smash of my face on pebbled concrete.

It's because I was afraid of not believing in God that I started going to Hendricks Chapel. I was lying half on and half off a beanbag chair in my dorm room leaking blood through my jeans and not giving a crap the pain was so bad when I thought I should probably start going to church and make sure God was real.

The first time I went, I hung near the back while three girls stood on a small stage holding broom handles to their mouths and lip syncing to a Sandy Patty song. After that a guy named Joe Karlya, who has remained a close friend, gave a short talk about something I don't remember. When the meeting ended, even though I was in the back and clearly keeping my distance, students quickly surrounded me. Smiles and handshakes. After spending a few minutes meeting them I grabbed a brownie from a table and left.

As I made my way back across campus to my dorm, evening had just about descended. Other than the uppermost still-light sky, there was a blue cast over everything, down the façades of the buildings and across the grass. I was glad I had gone and at the same time didn't want my friends to know. Students who came up to people on the quad to talk about Jesus belonged to Christian fellowships; they were strange, they were overly nice and didn't swear, and lip-synced to Sandy Patty.

In the end, those were the students who became my dearest friends. I started going to a Bible study and even a few retreats where I started thinking about things I'd been putting off thinking about since I was a kid. That semester God, and Christ, became real to me.

At one point I decided to talk to my philosophy professor about God. I made an appointment with him and went to the philosophy department where we both sat down at a small table in a common area, and I began to pontificate on God, and eternity, our minds and our souls, things he knew nothing about.

A few sentences in and he was already stifling a laugh. Barely. He was probably a PhD candidate, so he might have had his own insecurities, but just as soon as I began to talk, any confident zeal I'd had when I sat down with him zapped invisible like a mosquito on a bug light. I was trying to explain the importance of Old Testament prophesies when he said something I didn't understand and my eyes started to sting. I got the Qur'an and the Torah mixed up and told him if he looked up Isaiah in the Qur'an there were places that said the Messiah would be born in Bethlehem, and that maybe he could even talk about it in class sometime, at which point he started to laugh out loud and I became entirely confused and my stinging eyes started to water so that I tried to wrap up my incoherencies before the tears slid all the way down my cheeks. That's when another professor walked by and told him to shut up, which felt like God himself had passed by and whacked the back of his head with the guy's own unfinished dissertation.

I've embarrassed myself to no end in this life. But perhaps surprisingly, trying to talk to a philosophy professor about God wasn't one of my worst moments. Maybe it's because there was redemption when the other guy walked by and told him to shut up, or maybe it doesn't bother me so much because after all it was God I was talking about, and surely God was on my side. Regardless, I'm still glad I did it.

If I were to go back through my journals from our years battling Sweetboy's addiction, I'm sure they would read like hurricanes; winds so fierce they can fell trees with centers so calm the sky is blue. Most of my writing consisted of begging, once again, for the pain to end. I was looking for redemption, for the appearance of good, because my pain and longing and uncertainty felt out of my control, like one gust of bad news only meant another gust was on its way, so I prayed for peace, I prayed for God himself to show up and whack The Evil unconscious.

Eventually I learned to thank him. Thanking him became that blue sky in the middle of a hurricane and that's where I found the peace. Even though I still didn't know what was ahead, thanking him was a good batch better than a few milligrams of Xanax.

APPLE PIE

THERE ARE CERTAIN CIRCUMSTANCES in which I don't follow the rules. These circumstances will always have to do with nature, the wild, rocks and streams and lakes, areas that aren't defined by curbs and streetlights. If there are barriers around a live oak or a crystal stream, unless it's a privately owned area, my general attitude, if there's no danger involved, is *have at it*.

Once Rick and I brought Jules and Sweetboy to a state park. It was hot, and there was a gently rushing stream, one of those streams with light splitting through the trees and small areas where the water builds up into still, small pools. Streams like this can be so beautiful they hurt because there's something about you that limits you and makes it impossible to fully comprehend.

We sat on a rock and Jules and Sweetboy took off their shoes and dangled their feet in the water, then knees, then seemed to decide wet clothes were a small price to pay and sunk completely into one of the shallow pools. They climbed up on a rock and slipped in then climbed it again. They found a place where a small rush of water fell into a pool. We watched as they swam and climbed. They were eager in that stream, as though they had discovered something like mica, some kind of childhood gold only they understood.

I held Sweetboy's hand as we headed back to the car. He and Jules walked like cowboys to keep their wet clothes from rubbing. Sweetboy looked up at me and said, "Thanks! I think that's the most fun I've ever had!"

* * *

In our previous home, four blocks from the one we live in now, we had an old, half-dead apple tree in our backyard. It was gangly, with peeling bark and patches of bare wood like age spots, but there was one large trunk that still managed to produce apples. And the trunk was prolific; the apples came every fall, thumb-sized at first, clustered together like green rosettes on the branches, until they grew volume and pulp and it was magic how fast they grew. Then the yellow jackets came and hovered around the rotting ones on the ground.

Making something with a child can change you. Things that long ago became routine for an adult take on a clarity lost to freeway miles and bank lines years ago. Apples and Sweetboy did that for me.

One day, when he had just started preschool, I watched from the kitchen window, dish sponge in hand, as he ran across our backyard in that strange loping gait he had, one arm swinging helicopter-like as though to increase his speed. I cherished that run, but it would slowly disappear like so many things: Legos and play dough and forts in the living room. I watched as he stopped under the apple tree, picked up an apple, and threw it at the trunk. He bent down, picked up another one, turned it around until he found a good part, and timidly took a bite. He took another larger bite and then puckered his lips. The apples weren't the luscious ones families pick in orchards, zipped up in fleece jackets for an annual fall tradition. They were ugly and green and had wormholes and never got beyond the sour to become sweet reds. They always dropped prematurely. Sweetboy searched around in the grass until he found two more decent apples and ran back into the kitchen.

"Can we make a pie?"

I was hesitant. I didn't think there were enough good apples, without wormholes. I took the two he had; although small, one of them didn't have any holes or rot, the other one only had two or three dark spots. I looked at the clock. We had three hours until the girls got home.

"Alright, okay, we can try . . ." I went to the closet and pulled out a plastic bag. "Fill it up with as many good ones as you can find." He eagerly ran across the yard, bag billowing with his circling arm.

The rest of the afternoon we made pies. One large and one small. I stood at the counter slicing the bad parts out of the apples while Sweetboy stood on a chair and mixed sugar and flour and cinnamon, surrounded by bowls and measuring spoons and canisters, while the heat of the oven warmed the kitchen.

A few months earlier, when I was cleaning, I had pulled out a folded note from behind a radiator. It was old and yellow, and had been stuck behind the radiator for so long the folds were beginning to split. It had been written by a daughter to her mother who was living in the house at the time. The apple tree must have been lovely then and in its prime, pruned short with the middle low and flat the way they're supposed to be so that the branches grow out more than up and are easy to reach. The letter went on for two full pages about how Sarah so and so made her apple pies with unsifted flour, so the crusts weren't nearly as flaky as yours, mother. The daughter continued the apple pie diatribe by outlining the details of her own perfect pie making skills, having apparently learned them from her mother who still lived in the house—which was now our house—with the more-than-likely healthy and well pruned apple tree with juicy red apples in the backyard, which were now tiny green ones with holes, that we were about to press into patched together pie crusts.

That note stuck with me. It came from a time that I imagined to be perfect: a sunny, breezy fall day, a mother wearing a linen apron and a calf-length skirt. Laundry hanging outside on a line while children play Red Rover in the crisp air. Of course those imagined perfect moments weren't perfect. As there are today, there were wars and scraped knees and racism and birth defects and alcoholism. But I still can't help but think that long ago if that first little drop of morphine, wherever it originated, had never touched the first skin, thousands of people would have been saved from miles of pain.

But now, with Sweetboy across from me pressing out pie dough with his small palms, things did seem perfect. Even without Red Rover and laundry drying in the sun the world was awfully beautiful.

* * *

When he was young Sweetboy was particularly sensitive to food. I think if he had been our firstborn I would have been more on top of that—made sure he was trying new things, held off on the snack food, no sugar. But then a parent always regrets. It's one of those hapless parts of parenting.

The regrets: Our kids were all under two years apart and much of what I remember of those years was trying to do chores with Sweetboy on my hip; I was distracted by laundry and his sisters. I tried to keep the TV off as much as possible, and in the end I think this encouraged their creative tendencies, but as far as structure, other than naps and reading and bedtime, there wasn't much. Today they would probably be called "free range kids," and while I wholeheartedly agree with a good bit of free range for children, in retrospect I wonder if more structure would have prevented him from doing drugs. Hindsight, yes, but it's hard not to swing back around to those years now and imagine the "if onlys," where raising them would have been like clockwork: preschool, grade school, homework, youth group, sports, high school, friends, college, responsibility, independence. Parenting was supposed to be *if this, then that*. We would raise them right and they would be all right.

* * *

For me, maybe a little helicopter parenting would have been a good thing. It's very easy to blame myself for Sweetboy's drug use, even if it's a stretch. While at the time I felt that having the freedom to go out and wander the neighborhood was healthy for him, I wonder now if more structure would have been better. But I'm probably remembering selectively—I know there were certain times for homework and I was strict about bedtimes. Even now I judge my parenting. Years later I can still compare and contrast. I think about the families with the kids all lined up like the Von Trapp family, holding their soccer awards and college scholarships, and feel ashamed. Of course, blaming myself isn't okay—there is no one thing I did wrong that I can isolate and blame for my child eventually doing heroin. It's far more complicated than that, and there's an awful lot of kids growing up with an awful lot of love and plenty of food who sleep in cozy rooms with 100 percent down comforters on their beds and still struggle with addiction.

Addiction has been linked to many things, some well-known and some less so: impulsivity, nonconformity, social alienation, abuse, stress, abnormalities in dopamine levels, heritability, depression, phobias, anxiety, poverty, trauma. And then there are the lesser-known things: male, white, young, Asperger's, high IQ, and high birth weight. Like cancer, it rarely has one clear cause, but a handful of them, for example, heritability and phobia, or smart, isolated, and impulsive. Almost always, addiction is a comorbid disease, meaning it's combined with another disease. Morbid = affected by. Co = mutual. The overall disease is affected by mutual factors.

If Rick and I had genetic testing, and the whirling tubes of our blood spun out this or that faulty gene like a spitew of sand from the mouth and sent all kinds of banzai red lights blinking around the lab indicating our match was risky at best, would we have thought twice before we had children? I'm glad we didn't. I'm glad we had Sophie, and Jules, and Sweetboy.

✳ ✳ ✳

The food issue, although I told myself he would grow out of it, only got worse. Being a picky eater did not cause Sweetboy's addiction, but there is a link between picky eaters and anxiety and depression, and there's a strong correlation between anxiety and depression and addiction. There're things I remember now that, thinking back on, I find interesting; everything packed together like a tangled knot. Two bites of everything and then dessert turned into one bite of everything and then dessert, turned into Nature Valley granola bars an hour after lunch because he was hungry, turned into open boxes of chocolate covered Shoprite granola bars and artificially flavored fruit gummy snacks in the pantry. He liked sugar. That's what he wanted: sugar, only in different forms, snacks disguised as health food in brown paper packaging to ease my guilt.

Twice his desire for sugar could have killed him. The first time he was two and got into the pantry where I stored a bottle of chewable vitamins plus iron, something I dutifully gave him in hopes it would supplement his diet and prevent scurvy or whatever people get today when they don't eat enough fruits and vegetables. I found him on the kitchen floor with the empty plastic container that that very morning had been full. He was happy and sitting on his knees—that two-year-old position that seems to provide just enough temporary spring to quickly get them to whatever trinket or knob or switch looks particularly interesting at the time. Well-aware that vitamins plus iron in high amounts can be poisonous, I immediately took him to the emergency room where he sat on my lap for two hours sipping cherry-flavored charcoal to absorb the iron. He pooped green for a week.

The second time, he was three. He climbed up on the bathroom sink and got into the medicine cabinet, which is where the dangerous stuff is. Cough syrup with codeine. I assume he was after the sugar, not the codeine. He's told me he remembers climbing on the sink and getting into the cabinet, but that he didn't actually drink the cough syrup, just opened it and poured it down the drain. I'm sure he's right, that he didn't drink the cough syrup, but of course I needed to be on the safe side. In the emergency room they monitored him until the doctor was satisfied he hadn't poisoned himself, and sent us home.

Even as raw and bruised up as the apples were, our pies *were* good. And after that, for the next few years, we made them every fall. There was something about the underdone greenness that gave them the perfect amount of tart. We added a lot of sugar and the crusts didn't stretch like they were supposed to, so we always patched them together like play dough. I usually gave Sweetboy a small ceramic bowl to make his own pie. He would mix the cinnamon and sugar and play the crust into different shapes, licking his fingers every now and then. When he looked up, he would have a smear of sugary cinnamon ringing his mouth. I thought he was the sweetest boy I'd ever seen.

* * *

Before Jules was born I found a book about prayer by E. M. Bounds in a box in our basement. The first time I saw the book I thought E. M. Bounds was a woman. When I found out he was a man I was disappointed because I wanted to be one of those women who prays a lot and isn't afraid of anything, and I assumed I'd relate better to a woman than a man.

I imagined E. M. Bounds not only as a woman, but as a mother, sitting in a small, dark kitchen with a cream-colored linen tablecloth and a cup of tea. This is how I imagine Christians lived a century ago— with a cup of tea and an open Bible at the kitchen table. I once heard that Susanna Wesley, mother of John and Charles Wesley, would sometimes sit in a corner of the room, drape a cloth over her head, and pray. Her children weren't to disturb her when she had her head draped and bowed.

Susanna Wesley was unshakeable and I wanted to be like her so I asked God to make me like that, a woman sitting in the corner all hunched over praying.

LOCO

ONE AFTERNOON I borrowed a nail gun and made Sweetboy a sleeping loft. A nail gun is a powerful thing and, for me, a little addicting. I shot nails into every possible joinery and board. Every once and a while a nail would miss and ping off a wall or the floor or into the small hallway and then ricochet a couple times before landing on the carpet or flying down the stairs. I worked hard on the ladder, then nailed 2x4s for the platform for the mattress straight into the wall where I'd found some studs. I kept shooting in nails. I was obsessing over making it sturdy. From time to time Sweetboy came in and asked if I was done yet. He was excited; we'd gone to Home Depot that morning to pick out the wood together, but as the project had become more and more complicated, I'd grown silent in concentration. After checking in on the progress, he'd wander back outside to play. I'd woken up that morning, stared at the ceiling, and imagined what it would look like. I excitedly told Sweetboy my plan—my eyes were half bugged out I was so excited about it. Rick was traveling and I wanted it done before he got home. I made a railing to go around the platform, attached the ladder, rubbed walnut-colored stain into the whole thing and wiped it off with a dry rag, hauled a mattress up the ladder, and made the bed, crawling around trying to keep my head from hitting the ceiling as I tucked the sheets into the corners. When it was done Sweetboy and I stood back and looked at it. The loft was level and sturdy, but still. It was obvious I'd built it in a day. It was made of nailed together 2x4s with a coat of walnut stain haphazardly applied, but even with its uneven stain and nail holes and mattress too close to the ceiling, Sweetboy loved it. At least at first he loved it, until he gently told me it was hard to sleep so close to the ceiling and I pulled the mattress down and put it under the bed and made curtains to go around it like a fort. It smelled like Minwax for weeks. One day he jumped off the highest rung of the ladder and broke the ceiling light, which had cowboys with lassos painted on it. The room had a cowboy theme; there was a lamp with a shade that had cowboys on bucking broncos too.

When I felt good I made sleeping lofts and painted murals on our kitchen walls and chopped up trees with chainsaws. When we were staying in a hotel one time, I went into the bathroom so I wouldn't wake the kids and scribbled out a short story late into the night. When I read it the next day, it was terrible and I crumpled it up and threw it away. One very rainy day I grabbed a windbreaker and headed outside to walk Daisy the dog and then began to run. I couldn't stop, and I ran faster and faster until the beautiful, rainy, mid-level sky seemed to settle around me like mist. I ran in the street, Daisy loping along, through puddles and down alleys, and I would have kept going if I didn't fall. Daisy crossed in front of me and I tripped over the leash and went down. My elbow hit first and then my head, and like a stutter in the middle of a day I blacked out for a moment. I was a little dizzy as I walked home, and hours later half my arm was the color of eggplant. I have no doubt that if it were 1910 and I'd hiked up my skirts and run wildly through the muddy, horse dung covered streets, Rick would have had to tell me we were going for a Sunday carriage ride and then, bewildered, I'd find myself in front of a plain red brick building with a circular drive, at which point nurses would struggle me out of the carriage and into the building and hose me down before locking me in a room to wait until some surgeon, convinced of the science of it, would give me rubber to bite on and shock me three feet toward the ceiling, or ether me half dead and scoop out an eighth of my brain in an attempt to make me sane again. Things are different now.

When our kids were babies, I would put on Elvis Costello and dance around the living room with them, around and around, while they giggled and smiled. Other times I would lie on the couch barely able to move while they watched Sesame Street and Mr. Rogers.

When I felt bad it was like a continual hiss that erased future, not *a* future or *my* future, but just plain future, as though it wouldn't exist for anyone anymore, least of all me. Life became meaningless. I was never a homeroom mom or made sure my kids got involved in soccer or ballet. Natural peanut butter notwithstanding, I didn't always feed them well; they ate a lot of frozen pizza. I occasionally raged, whether from steroidal-like hypomanic RPMs or depression, I don't know. In Joan Didion's memoir, *The Year of Magical Thinking*, which chronicles the year after her husband's death, she mentions "the shallowness of sanity, of death." Our meaningless death, our eventual disappearance that drives us or stalls us—I can easily circle those words as my own. Death is shallow but sane, but then it's also deep and sane. This dichotomy becomes sanity; our meaningless, meaningful death is forecast by a meaningless, meaningful life.

I don't know if being bipolar made parenting more difficult for me than most—maybe some days it did and some days it didn't, but knowing the highs and lows my moods were capable of made it necessary to always remember, as Hebrews 13:8 says, "Jesus Christ is the same yesterday and today and forever." So whether I couldn't get out of bed or I was dancing with my babies, I knew the God who made the trees and molecules and mountains and subterranean currents wouldn't disappear even though evil eventually would. I was sane like the atheist is sane in his consistency, who lives in the same world that I do, but watches his parents die and wars destroy the earth and sees no God, so sees no hope. Given the chance, I'm sure we'd commit each other to a sanatorium; we'd end up at some behavioral-research-science-neurological-mental-institution and have our tea together and be so medicated it wouldn't matter that we both thought the other one was birdbrained.

There are many books about bipolar illness, but I've never come across one written from the perspective of a mother with the disease. They're usually written by their adult children. Bipolar illness translates into some terrific writing—crazy mothers in the middle of the night painting the trees in the front yard white, that sort of thing. My own grandmother dragged her oil paints to the basement and covered the walls with oak trees. I think she spent most of her days down there.

Mental illness brings with it a unique challenge for mothers. Before I was treated, if I was hypomanic, I thought I was the greatest mother in the world. If I was depressed, I thought I was the worst mother in the world. But the truth is I was neither; I was a fine mother—a loving mother. I was a good mother. At times I'm still tempted to ruminate on the ways that I failed Sweetboy, but that's assuming I had more control than I did which is a pretty solipsistic way of looking at things.

But my children were my blessings. Every day they gave me life. Every night, depressed or manic or perfectly normal, Sophie, Jules, and Sweetboy climbed on my bed and I read to them: *Winnie the Pooh*, *Huckleberry Finn*, and the warmth of their bodies gave me peace like the Holy Spirit gives peace.

NAMES

Few parents can say the word *heroin*. It took me a long time to say it. A lot of people misspell *heroin* as *heroine*, which seems about right because heroin is like a heroine in disguise; it swoops in to save the day and take away whatever feels bad but ends up killing the one who needed saving. A wolf in sheep's clothing. When I was taking notes for this book, I just wrote *H*. The letter *H* was easier to put down on the page. Less combustible, like if I held off on the rest of the letters, then this apotheosis of evil would somehow fizzle out to nothing before it could drag another victim into some alley with determined tufts of grass growing from cracks of asphalt and cement like wormy green blood. There are a lot of words that are useful as substitutes for the H word. The vague word *drugs*, for example, works well, but leaves too wide a spectrum of possibilities, including less noxious substances like marijuana. You can say "hard drugs," which is better, but it's still a mash-up. What? Meth? Crack cocaine? I've thought a lot about whether it sounds worse to have a child who does heroin or meth. If given a choice, as a mother, would I rather have to say my child was addicted to heroin or meth? I'm still not sure. I know both kinds of parents. I think parents must spend time thinking about this when their kid's either an H kid or an M kid. Either way, both the H kid and the M kid swim like spelunkers through deep caverns far beyond the reach of the sun, and it's impossible to know whether they'll ever make it back.

There are locusts flattened within the pages of the Bible. John the Baptist eats them with wild honey in the desert and stubborn Pharaoh and his glorious Egypt become infested with them. In Nahum 3:15 it says, "The sword will cut you off. It will devour you like the locust." In Proverbs 30:27, "The locusts have no king, yet all of them march in rank." Locusts swarm. As innocent as they might be singularly, en masse they are a killing machine. They destroy living things. They destroy food. They ruin future harvests. As small as they are, in a multitude they become a monster. In Madagascar there have been swarms so destructive they would warrant a state of emergency in America. Their swarming bodies turn the air into TV static.

But in the second chapter of the book of Joel, God says, "I will restore to you the years that the swarming locust has eaten."

The God of miracles who can make camels go through the eyes of needles can also redeem years of pest-eaten fields that produced nothing. This is a true thing. He *wants* to redeem every day that drugs have taken from a life; the lost happiness and relationships and growth. At one point I began praying the Lord's Prayer, especially the part that says, "Your will be done, on earth as it is in heaven," because his will is restoration. The whole Bible is about healing and restoration, *always*. He *wants* harvests to be plentiful and all the flying bugs with their overlapping droning voices to vanish like the mist vanishes as the sun rises. And isn't this what we all hope for? Not just that God will save our children and the people we love, but that he will turn every dark night and empty bed into some as-of-now-unknown beautiful thing? Yes. So it's for these things we pray.

* * *

There's an area of Philadelphia that bears the misleading name Kensington, as though it's a place of rolling green hills with stone markers and sheep and elderly men walking the grounds carrying leather satchels and fishing tackle. Kensington in Philadelphia also goes by the name Badlands, and according to the Urban Dictionary, is "a very VERY dangerous area of North Philly. The best and most reliable place in the tristate area to pick up really decent heroin, crack, powder coke, benzos, Suboxone, needles, weapons, prostitutes or whatever else you might need." This is word for word what the Urban Dictionary says. (If you have a kid who does drugs, don't look up things in the Urban Dictionary because it will turn your day inside out with the seams showing.)

Kensington is also called Heroin City. The most active part of it consists of a small triangular area under elevated train tracks. There are shootings every day. There are crack houses and shooting galleries and women getting raped and sometimes killed. There are shrines to the dead in small overgrown areas where row houses are missing: melted candles, stuffed animals. Most of them are tributes put there by friends. Sometimes by enemies: R. I. P. Bum, one shrine says. The Evil is loud and obnoxious, like he's just so giddy with excitement over another dead body that he can't hold back and pounds stakes into the ground in honor of another victory. Hate is his mistress and he finds her beautiful. The police don't bother going into Kensington because nothing they do there will make a difference anyway. Addicts walk around with their teeth half out and faces sucked in, covered in red meth acne, or with tracks up their wiry arms and anywhere else it's possible to stick a needle: necks, legs, feet, ankles. I don't know anything about the combinations of drugs these addicts have addled together, but apparently a good cocktail can achieve great effect. Xanax mixed with other pills and snorted, that sort of thing. Once Sweetboy told me that people walk around the streets calling out whatever they have to sell: "Xanies" (Xanax), "Subs" (Suboxone). I've also heard there are two main dealers that rule Kensington, one black and one white. If you're black you get your drugs on one side of the street, if you're white, on the other. I've read that real community works better than AA or even prescribed medications in helping addicts get sober. That sounds right to me. Replacing fake love with real love. I wish I could take every addict in the world and replace opiate's false love with human love.

There's also a park in Kensington. It's called McPherson Park. There's a library in the middle of it that's surrounded by grassy areas on all four sides, and even though you're in the middle of a city, if you stand there on a clear night you can see the stars.

GLASS HALF EMPTY

WHEN SWEETBOY was five years old we had a run-in with a couple semi-trucks. We never hit them and we didn't crash, but I still call it a run-in because even though it didn't cause physical pain, it caused emotional pain.

We were in our red minivan driving to DC on Interstate 95 to meet Rick at a conference where he was speaking. I was in the middle lane and there were trucks on both sides of us. It was about 10:00 in the morning, that time of day when truck drivers seem to be making up time, driving fast and aggressively. Sophie was in the way back reading and Jules and Sweetboy were in the middle seats. Jules had been complaining about something, I don't remember what, when the van suddenly slowed as though I'd just run into something like a barrier of cotton. We were still moving, but slow, very slow. Semis were on either side and in back of us. There were no cars or trucks ahead, but my foot was already pressed to the floor and still, we were barely moving. There wasn't much I could do but hope we wouldn't get rear-ended.

It only took a few seconds for the trucks to pull ahead and the one on my rear to switch lanes and pass. A few more cars went by on my right; a space opened up, turn signal, switch lanes, turn signal, pull off on shoulder. But by the time I pulled off the road I was shaking. I'd yelled for the kids to be quiet, and they were. The car was silent, but I was shaken up and having a hard time breathing. I'm not sure why it rattled me so much. I'm a confident driver. At that point I was worried about how I'd get in touch with Rick since I didn't have a cellphone. Either way, I started to cry.

It was hot. Cars and trucks were barreling by on my left, causing the strong force of air every time they passed to jiggle the car. I'd pulled off next to some woods, one of those places on highways where parents pull over so they can work their kids' pants down and hold them over the grass so they can pee. Next to the trees, there was a five foot high swath of dead, yellowed vegetation that had been sprayed into a wilted mess with pesticides. I waited for a long pause in the traffic and quickly climbed out of the car.

Why an interstate in suburban America suddenly became my sortie of angst, I have no idea. Worst case, I flag someone to call a tow truck and call Rick when I get to the station, but I continued to shake. And cry. It was hot, I was sweating, the kids were in the car, and I felt out of control.

When I slid open the door to the van Sweetboy stepped out first, and this for some reason became for me one of those sailing maneuvers of life; a tack left or tack right to go forward. It was an ugly necessity for me to understand how much my worry—and times of depression—had affected him, because when I saw him he looked as though my own fear had jumped into the air and sparked a hot coal of fear somewhere in his own diaphragm.

He was crying. There was also a look about him, like he was looking for assurance, but knew I wasn't the place to get it. He wore tan cargo shorts and a green T-shirt with tiny horizontal cream-colored stripes and he was crying. I bent down and hugged him. *Oh Sweetboy, it's fine. Everything's fine. You don't need to worry. There's no reason for me to worry either, okay? I don't know why I was worrying.*

Another driver was kind enough to stop, and I used his cellphone to call Rick and a tow truck. Long day, but of course everything ended up fine. I did my best to keep Sweetboy close, but in the end there was no need—he was playing with his sisters and joking around.

In trauma, the memory is so vivid it's like it's pressed between glass slides and slid under a microscope to be studied later. Like so many people, I have my own vivid traumatic moments, and most of them I would consider universally traumatic; anyone would find them traumatic. However, the person who experiences the trauma defines the trauma and that day, when I realized that I had caused Sweetboy's fear, while it might seem silly to some, was actually traumatic to me. I remember every color and reflection of sun and expression on his face when I slid open the van door, right down to the gray pebbles that made up the shoulder of the interstate.

I have a drawing that Sweetboy gave me when he was young. It's on yellow paper and is drawn in black pen. There's a person in a boat holding a fishing rod. The word WORRY is attached to the end of the line and hangs just above the water. When he gave it to me, I knew right away that he'd drawn it to illustrate the verse in the Bible, in 1 Peter 5:7, where it says, "Casting all your anxieties on him, because he cares for you," and that he drew it for me because he didn't want me to worry anymore.

SETTLING IN

When Sweetboy was twelve, and the girls were fourteen and sixteen, we made the long drive up Interstate 95 from Florida. Having moved to Florida a year earlier, we were moving back. Rick was resting and I was driving. Sweetboy was in the back of the van rolling a mini finger skateboard along the car window, pretending to fly over jumps, and kept trying to pop an Ollie—a stunt that he would soon learn to do on a real skateboard as he glided down the street in long uneven swaths like the hem of a flowing skirt. He was probably on a skateboard when he made his way down to the highway with a boy up the street and spray painted SMACK on an underpass. I passed the graffiti on my way to CVS. He had to have painted it. Although I never asked him, the letters looked like the same letters I'd seen on so many of his notebooks and even on a skate ramp in the garage. I had no idea what smack was. Back then heroin was still a foreign thing.

Before we moved to Florida we lived in another house about a half mile from this one. We sold that house, thinking the move would be permanent, but then moved back after a series of unfortunate events. (It was the year of the hurricanes, the rats, the lone duck that we found one morning in our living room, the foundation that needed lifting, the water that burst through the ceiling, the possums, the rats, and the rats.)

The duck was a fluke, the hurricanes not so much, and I won't bother going into the rats; we had them. By the third hurricane the kids had grown used to the drill. We slept in the living room—the lowest part of the house—and they hauled down a few of their most treasured things, figuring that if the house blew apart they'd at least have something. Sophie brought her collection of Jane Austen books, Jules—who by then had taught herself Elvish—carried a five-foot cardboard Gandalf down the stairs, and Sweetboy put a leash on Daisy the dog and coaxed her to lie down next to his sleeping bag. Rick found the duck waddling around the living room one morning before it freaked out and escaped, shattering a glass window on its way out. Rick prayed the enormous tree in our front yard wouldn't fall on the house in a storm, and I prayed for a new place to live.

We purchased the house we live in now having never seen it. I'd made a trip up to Pennsylvania to find one but after wandering through a handful of raised ranches and split-levels that sold even as I walked out the front door, I flew back empty-handed. When this house unexpectedly came on the market we didn't bother flying up. We mailed a check, packed up the van, and left.

We all settled down and accepted our fate for the next ten hours. It was a long drive and the kids were tired. Somewhere in Georgia or South Carolina Sweetboy's finger skateboard disappeared in one of the minivan's many crevices, and at any one time two or three of us of were sleeping. It was a very dull, very long trip. By the time we got to our town there were remnants of meals from McDonalds and Subway littering the van: stray French fries, a plastic bag stuffed with miscellaneous food wrappers, ineffective plastic knives and crumpled napkins.

When we reached our town it was like our brains woke up again. We stuck our faces to the windows and gawked at the place we thought we'd said goodbye to forever. We grew silent. We made our way down the main street with the 1800s row houses, the brick sidewalks, the library with Bayard Taylor's tribute to Goethe etched in a stained glass window: *The man who, most of men / Heeded the parable from lips divine / And made one talent ten.* And then the trees—my beloveds—bursting through the sidewalks and mussing up the bricks like they were all too eager to welcome us home.

When we finally pulled in the driveway and saw our house for the first time, it seemed to emanate a totemic power—as though the porous orange bricks were sucking in the fall air. It was a personification, a face, a relative, someone we knew well but had never met.

The real estate agent had left the front door half open to welcome us. After I put the car in park we remained silent for a moment and I leaned my head over the dashboard and peered out the windshield. Then Jules said she needed a big room for her drum set.

They all climbed out and ran to the front door. I followed behind while Rick gathered up things in the car. Sophie said, "I get the biggest room. I'm the oldest and I didn't want to move back anyway."

"I need a place for my drum set."

"I have a queen bed. You only have a twin," Sophie said.

"I need a place for my drum set."

"You already said that, Jules."

"But I do."

For some reason I felt almost greedy as I stood on the sidewalk and looked at the house. Sweetboy had Daisy with him, and as he went inside, he kept petting her and explaining to her it was her new home. Rick was still unloading the car. The house was a brick Cape Cod with two dormers. The white front door was peeling paint and the wrought iron railings on either side of the steps were rusting. To the left of the door the large bay window with the curved panes of glass mildly reflected the sinking sun but also looked dark in the way that a just closed store is dark. The window was expansive and beautiful and I knew immediately it would be my favorite part of the house. I don't remember when I began looking at the night sky through it, staring at Orion's Belt and praying for our kids, but I knew it would be important, that the house would be dull and meaningless and not alive without the window. An old oak tree extended over the roof and there were dead branches littering the yard. Sticks were in the gutters and some of the gutters were loose. Glazing on the windows was chipping off and any areas where there should have been wood—the sides of the dormers, the front of the garage—had been covered in white aluminum siding that was beginning to turn gray. The cement slabs of the front walk had popped up a few inches and there were two tiny, hand-sized porch lights on either side of the front door. For a moment I felt light-headed, struck by the reality that we had bought this house with its ugly orange brick and the oak tree and the branches sliding down the roof, and there was no way to bail. I looked up at it soaking in sun with the door half open and the uneven slabs of cement half stuck in the earth.

Inside, the living room was to the left and had a large stone fireplace with a keystone above it. Off the living room was a short hallway with two bedrooms and a pink and black tiled bathroom. The small kitchen was at the back of the house and had forest green cabinets and a linoleum floor that had split down the middle, a puckered seam like a stuck zipper. I went upstairs where there was another bath and two bedrooms under the eaves with slanted ceilings, and as I went into the room on the right, light from the dormer window stretched long across the floor and hit the opposite wall. The room was filled with light and had rows of shelves built into one of the walls. It immediately became my favorite room in the house. In fact, right now as I write I'm sitting in a chair in that same sunny room with the dormer and the light that floods the floor and hits the opposite wall every afternoon. It's a peaceful room. Most of my books are stuffed into the built-in bookcase, slid tight into the rows and squeezed into the spaces above them.

Both of the upstairs rooms had half doors under the eaves that led to crawl spaces where insulation fell from the rafters and nails poked through the wood overhead where the roofing shingles had been nailed in. The closets were big, the floors were wood—if a little uneven—and I made my way through the rooms inspecting corners and closets and fixtures, every angle and every hinge. Downstairs I heard Sweetboy running around yelling to his sisters and Daisy's nails clicking on the wood floors. He ran up the stairs and peered into the bathroom before going into the adjoining room on the right, my favorite room, this room, the room with the sun, and opened the small door that led to the crawl space. "Your room," I said, smiling.

Sophie and Jules quickly claimed the downstairs bedrooms and even though Jules ended up with the smaller one, I pointed out that the smaller one had a special nook that was the perfect place for a drum set; she was happy about that. The wood floors, the dormers, the garage with the breezeway connecting to the kitchen, the French doors and the patio and a yard that seemed to stretch back acres with an enormous weeping birch tree. The house was tossed to us from a thousand miles away with its remnants of 1980s hunter green and floral valances, fixtures calcified and beginning to rust, a basement wrapped in warped 1970s paneling. I was in love.

* * *

A few months after we moved into the house, we decided to refinish the downstairs floors. It was a herculean task and part of the deal was that while they were being refinished we had to climb up a ladder and enter through Sweetboy's bedroom window so we wouldn't make footprints on the living room floor. It was difficult to get through the window because when you struggled to step over the sill it felt a lot like the ladder was going to detach from the house and you'd find yourself falling in a slow arch backwards, helplessly waiting until your back and then your head hit the driveway. Eventually it rattled us enough to figure out a way to use the front door instead. We made a makeshift ramp from the threshold of the door to the stairs, essentially making a bridge with a thick piece of plywood.

While the floors were being done I worried about the noxious smell of polyurethane that was wafting upstairs—I worried about the chemicals. I opened the kids' windows and put fans in them to circulate as much fresh air as possible. Now, when I'm Monday morning quarterbacking, wondering what we could've done differently for Sweetboy, I think about that smell and the poison of poly-everything floating around and wonder if it could have done something to our children, that maybe it caused their still rapidly developing brains to mutate a handful of neurons into sneaky little things that blocked pathways like tollgates, for endorphins, dopamine, serotonin, whatever a young brain needs. Someday we'll probably find out that tempera paint is poison like Agent Orange is poison, like the mosquito-killing fog that used to come from trucks slowly driving through neighborhoods is poison. We slept with the windows open. Is there a metaphor in all of this?

That fall Rick painted the house white.

One day I came home to find him on the grass with his head in his hands. He was leaning against the house and a ladder was on the ground behind the bushes. He was breathing hard, and when he looked up I could see long scratches on his elbows and hands.

I knelt down next to him. "Are you okay?"

He put his head back down, breathing slowly.

"What happened?"

"I fell. It was stupid, I stood on the top rung," he said, then slowly got onto his knees, stood up, and I followed him into the kitchen.

The ladder had slid out from under him when he stepped on the top rung in an attempt to reach the brick above Sweetboy's window. I don't know how long he had sat there in the grass, or if the scratches were from the brick or the ladder or the bushes, but it was a bad fall. He was in pain. Sometimes my mind goes yo-yo on me and I can see everything as prophetic, like the whole experience was a portent of a deeper pain Rick would one day experience; trying to paint above Sweetboy's window, sliding down the wall like a rock climber who's lost his grip. When I look back now, some of the most benign things can feel loaded with suggestive meaning.

Rick left the chimney for last, and because the roof has a steep pitch, he had to run fast up the shingles to the peak and hold on while he painted. If he didn't hold on he would begin to slide. He ran up, he ran down, dipping his brush in a can of white paint with each trip.

There were buckets and brushes and aluminum ladders. We were bruised and pinched and scraped. Daisy the dog disappeared for three days and then came back. It was hot and then it was cool and the house slowly turned white. From the sidewalk, the upstairs dormers were like eyes, and the front door an open mouth, the ramp up like a long tongue.

Six years later we would find Sweetboy, blue and barely breathing, in his upstairs room with the light that stretches across the floor. Rick would pound on his chest to try to get him to breathe.

SMOKING

THESE DAYS when a kid says "smoke" they often don't mean cigarettes. It took me a while to understand this. It was Jules who found out first that Sweetboy was smoking weed, and it was Sophie who told us. He was in youth group the night she told us. I got in the car and drove straight to the church.

I went around back and banged on the door to the youth group until someone let me in, walked quickly down the hall to where they were meeting, stood at the door, angrily signaled for Sweetboy to come, and practically yanked him into the hallway even as the youth pastor was up on the stage with a few high school kids who were laughing hysterically. My reaction was visceral, almost strangely so. Even though a lot of kids will try smoking weed, for some reason I knew even then that Sweetboy was at a higher risk for addiction, that for him there would be no "experimenting" with drugs, that like a bear sniffing a dumpster in the middle of the night, he'd keep going back. Once outside I shoved him forward, toward the car. "Stupid," I said. "What a stupid, stupid, idiot thing to do . . ." I wasn't raging. I was absolutely in my right mind, just angry as hell.

A few miles from our home, where the Brandywine River widens and deepens, there's a rope swing. Next to the swing are a handful of cracked white resin chairs and a small fire pit. Discarded beer bottles and soda cans are scattered around in the bushes. That's where Sophie found him after Jules told her he was smoking weed. Not sure of what to do, she picked up him and his friends, drove them to youth group, and came home and told us. I'm sure it was hard for her—she took the hit, not Jules, for ratting on Sweetboy. The kids had some kind of un-stated code—the information they shared with each other we weren't always privy to—and at the time I thought it was probably a good thing. Even though I imagine much of their talk was misjudgments and complaints about Rick and me because of the camaraderie they shared in light of being the only three people in the world with Rick and me as their parents. *Oh the misery*, they might have grumbled to each other on a bad day, and then when the winds changed, breathed in an At-lantean suck of air that could only come from their same inherited strength. They needed each other, and no one else could meet that need except each other. It always seemed to me good parenting was as much about being quiet as it was about saying the right thing. Not that I was presumptuous enough, even then, to give parenting advice, at least not without a very emphatic *of course I may be wrong*.

* ✳ *

There are a lot of different opinions regarding the legalization of mari-juana, and I know the tide is quickly turning toward legalization in many states, but from my vantage point I've come to believe legalizing marijuana would ultimately harm our kids; the bottom line being that—like alcohol—legalizing it would give them greater access to it.

My views are based mostly on the circumstantial. I've watched kids who are predisposed to mental illness have psychotic breaks after smoking, and evidence suggests a strong correlation between smoking marijuana and serious, lifelong psychiatric conditions, and while I didn't used to, I think it *can* be a gateway drug, if only because a kid might be more likely to hang out with and be influenced by other kids inclined to try a few pills from their parent's medicine cabinet or crack open a couple Adderalls and sniff them.

I think it can be deceptive, that marijuana can stone kids ignorant and when they're ignorant it can muffle the common sense that knows a little pill here or a little sniff there can ultimately change whether they end up surrounded by people they love and who love them, or with a pain in their shoulder from lying on cement all night. This is how it can turn out for some, for those who have a certain handful of genes passed through generations that stand there involuntarily saluting whatever new substance is traveling through their veins. The genetic message being four beers are preferable to one and six preferable to four and Xanax brings it all together, but oxycodone does it best. I realize that statistically speaking, the large majority of those who smoke weed don't go on to use hard drugs, but because I know personally so many kids who seem to have entered into a life of drug use when they were young by being at the right place at the right time with the right cannabis, it's hard not to apply the discussion primarily to them.

David Sheff, author of *Beautiful Boy*, a memoir about his son's meth addiction, believes that marijuana should be legalized. But he also makes the point that it's not harmless. In an interview with NPR, he states:

> I support legalization. But there are a lot of people that support legalization who say things that are just wrong. They say that marijuana should be legalized because it's harmless, you know, it's

natural, and no one has ever died from marijuana, you can't get addicted to marijuana—those things are all untrue. Marijuana is not innocuous. There's a lot of research—again, this especially pertains to teenagers. Their brains are developing, marijuana changes the development. . . . The effects include problems with their cognition and memory and motivation and there's some evidence that it even lowers IQ. So, I think that we need to legalize pot so we can start a new conversation and deal with this for what it is. It's not a criminal problem and shouldn't be treated as a criminal problem. It's a health problem. So we need to focus on education and not punishment. ("David Sheff On Addiction: Prevention, Treatment and Staying 'Clean,'" March 27, 2013, NPR)

* * *

When I pulled Sweetboy out of youth group that night I assumed it was the first time he'd smoked. Even so, a few weeks later, I searched his room to make sure there wasn't a stray pipe or miniature tumbleweed tucked in a plastic baggie lying around. I hunched through the small door to the crawlspace—where he used to hide when playing hide and seek—and ferreted around, pushing aside his cast-off childhood things: cardboard boxes cut into tiny skate ramps, G.I. Joes, G.I. Joe's parachute and broken plastic Jeep, notebooks and half-finished drawings. I looked for a pipe or a plastic sandwich bag. A bong?— I assumed paraphernalia had changed since I was a kid. It was dark in the crawlspace and the insulation fell from the rafters, dropping stingers of fiberglass over the wood floor. I felt around in the dark, found nothing, but kept searching. I wanted to make sure. If anything was there, I wanted to find it, if only a few thumb-sized clumps of Mary Jane lying lonely in the corner.

Then, about to give up, I saw the edge of something clear and plastic tucked into the insulation and pulled out a two-liter Coke bottle. One side was smashed in and it crackled as I turned it around. There was no cap, and a pen without a cartridge was duct taped into a small hole on one side. I must have known it was a bong in a matter of seconds, but for some reason I was still confused—perhaps more confused by the reality that my son was still smoking weed, that it might have become a habit, than confused about what the thing was. Still, strangely (because what else could it possibly be?), I hoped for the best and searched online for similar images—and they were plentiful. (1) Hollowed out pen, (2) foil, (3) one-liter Coke bottle. The ingenious homemade bong. After that, every object in his room became suspect; when you realize you've been habitually underestimating drug use and all of the attending paraphernalia that goes with it, it's easy to swing in the other direction; a vaporizer on the floor next to a bed in winter becomes a contraption capable of making meth or an extractor that magically sucks opiates out of over-the-counter cough syrup. A mother's imagination can run wild.

However, even with the homemade bong, and his eventual use of harder drugs, Sweetboy was still the unique, gifted boy I knew—he *wasn't* like other kids who did drugs. I think every parent of a struggling child should know that their own kid *isn't* like the other kids who do drugs. Same issue, different souls entirely, and in no way does God lump them all together. In fact, even though I use it, I don't really like the term *addict*. It says in the Bible that God will give us each a white stone with a new name on it (Revelation 2:17), and there's certainly joy in that; I can't wait to know what mine is. Maybe it will carry within it explanations for the myriad questions I've had about myself, and all the ones I haven't, like the Myers–Briggs times one million. We sometimes attach words to names to reveal more about who we are; my husband has a PhD after his name, my blog tells people I'm a writer. We don't attach words to our given names that dull us into nothing more than one ant in a colony of them. An ant is an anti-personality, and God wants us to understand that he made us unique, and who we are is even more beautiful than "and then there was light, and there was day." Referring to someone as an addict is like hiding a beautiful person behind a pee test and a dose of Suboxone. They aren't addicts, they're Jason, or Becca, or Nathan. They are the kids who pop ollies on skateboards, draw that huge tree in your backyard, and burn up the soccer field.

It was after I found the bong that I began looking for an ulterior motive, an underlying reason Sweetboy had gotten to where he was, an explanation. I wanted people to admire him because he was worth admiring, to know his precious heart even though it wasn't always visible. This is what parents do, even as we're angry, even as we begin to accept the reality; we protect our children, and part of protecting them, and ourselves, is coming up with an explanation, something outside of themselves that negatively influenced them, because it's hard for us to imagine that it's their fault. We remember them as innocent children. Sweetboy's boyhood innocence is what I was constantly trying to claim again, and if I knew what caused him to get involved with drugs, I thought it would be possible to walk things back again, to where he hung out with Rick and skateboarded sans weed. This was my thinking at the time.

I smashed the plastic bottle and yanked out the pen. He'd always loved making things.

THE LOST BOYS

EVEN NOW I'm not sure how or when the first boy ended up in one of our spare rooms, tucked in at two in the morning, snug in the winter as the heat kicked on, or with windows open in summer, the early barks of dogs in the morning.

I called them The Lost Boys because they reminded me of the boys in *Peter Pan* looking for adventure and endlessly fighting the ugly, wooden-legged Captain Hook. I grew to love The Lost Boys. Every single one of them.

And Rick did too. I have to believe that somehow our love for them made a difference, even if we weren't always able to pull them back into the light as they were caught tangled by ankle or leg and ignorant of the things trying to tug them under. We tried to be here for them if they wanted to talk, and if they needed someplace to live that was away from The Evil, we gave them beds to sleep in. We fed them. We took this very seriously because we loved them.

They weren't lost like a kid wandering the streets is lost; most of them had homes of their own and parents who loved them, but for whatever reason our home became a magnet and they trickled in one by one.

It all began when Jules asked if she and Brian and Kelli, two of her friends, could clean out the upstairs of our garage. It's a large unfinished area with rafters like whale bones and nails from the asphalt roof sticking through the wood. There are stairs at the back and plenty of room to stand up, and on either end—at the front of the garage and at the back—there are windows. The window at the front, facing the street and our driveway, is round and has chipping paint and glazing coming loose, but it still lets in light. There's an enormous oak tree in the backyard that still has a rope swing that Sweetboy and I hung one afternoon when he was in sixth grade. The branch was so high we couldn't get the rope over it, so we tied a rock to one end and tried unsuccessfully to throw it over; the rock kept slipping out and we couldn't throw the rope more than five feet into the air. Eventually Sweetboy put a ladder under the tree and I found a clamp that stayed on the rope. It took him a few times to get it over, but he did. The tree has a disfigured trunk that twists around itself and has re-grown at an angle, reaching up and over the roof of the garage. The trunk is heavy and overgrown and when it's in leaf it spreads over the roof like it's either protecting or threatening it. The shingles of the garage have sprouted moss and are littered with twigs and branches. Sometimes after a storm the branches are the size of arms or legs, resting quietly like they hope you didn't see them fall.

I said yes to Jules fixing up the space because I thought it would be good for them to have somewhere to hang out, out of the house but close enough for us to keep track of what was going on. I didn't know that Jules had already begun to smoke cigarettes. She'd recently gotten back from a school retreat. I imagined those retreats to be life changing: little talks on goodness and thankfulness and kids sharing about what they were thankful for. I imagined them all sitting around a fire with the sparks floating up into the dark. I always imagine fires without the irritation of the smoke changing directions until it stings your eyes and you have to move to the other side, upwind of the breeze, probably for the same reason I picture sailboats always moving at eight knots, healed over, and not stagnant in the doldrums with the sails windless and flapping and not able to force the boat even ten feet forward. I idealized everything at that point. High school. Sports and proms and guitars in the evenings.

I was in the kitchen the night they fixed up the garage. They started by hauling chairs up from the basement and through the kitchen. They were even able to get a large green one from the basement and then to the garage and up the stairs. I'd found the chair at Salvation Army a year earlier and once I got it home it occurred to me that it was the ugliest chair I'd ever seen. I was happy to see it go. After the chair came armloads of stuff: Jules's guitar, string lights, some kind of old Nintendo and a small TV, a coffee table, another guitar, a box of art supplies, one of my own oil paintings that I had abandoned halfway through. I hated that oil painting like I hated the green chair.

There was a Bob Marley vibe early on. There was art. They hung tapestries and Chinese lanterns and dragged up an old rug. It was all very Jack Kerouac but without the drugs; I truly don't think there were drugs early on. They took Polaroid pictures and thumbtacked them to the rafters. They drew on the wood with white chalk: "Wake up!" and "Art isn't something you do, it's a state of mind." Jesus was up there too. There was a paint by number that someone had hung above the round window and I thought good, he can watch over them, he'll tolerate their immaturities and breathe the Holy Spirit like a smoke. In the painting—it's still up there—Jesus is holding his hands gently out and it looked like he was blessing them. His face seemed too solemn to me, like he was angry, so one afternoon when no one was there I took a dab of acrylic paint and touched up the corners of his mouth. The dab of paint worked; it changed his whole countenance. Jesus was now smiling, but not in a snarky way, in a way that said, *I love you,* and not only that, now it looked like he was almost laughing, not because something was funny, but maybe because he was happy. He seemed really happy to me after I fixed his mouth.

One of Jules's friends was a musician; he played the marimba at school and had a voice that soaked into the walls and then echoed back in soft, perfectly pitched notes. By that time our house was accustomed to the idioms of young people, and tolerant of their ideologies regarding anti-slick, anti-megachurch, come as you are, the hell with structure, in light of the general atmosphere of the place. I let them carve their names into a coffee table and tack close-up Polaroids of their mouths leaking hookah smoke like misty bubbles under water to the dining room walls. It wasn't that I didn't care what the house looked like; I did. It was more because it felt right; it fit the vibe. There was a freedom in these things, a non-constraint that seemed to leak from the walls, like a buffer from the outside world that allowed us to know them better. In the winter there was always a fire in the living room, and The Lost Boys would talk about the world and themselves and other people and faith. Eventually, they started reading the Bible together. I put Jenga blocks in a bowl on the kitchen table and they wrote their names and made designs with magic markers on them. I would come into the kitchen and sometimes it would be completely quiet as they wrote on the blocks.

That first night Jules and her friends hauled everything up to the room above the garage, she came into the kitchen and said, "We're calling it The Chill Spot."

"I like it. That's a cool name." I was glad they'd done it. It would be a place to talk, to get deeper. They would talk about art and music. They would talk about God.

"Come look at it!"

I followed her into the garage and up the stairs. Even as I walked up I could see that the lights they had strung across the beams had transformed the place. There were swags of them stapled to the wood like curtains. They had found a rug somewhere and sectioned off a sitting area at the end of the room where a large red tapestry that I didn't recognize hung. The two guitars leaned neatly against the wall under the round window and the TV and Nintendo were off to one side. Brian and Kelli sat next to each other squished into the green chair. There was a small CD player on a crate with a pile of CDs next to it and Coldplay's *A Rush of Blood to the Head* played quietly. The music had the same effect the string lights had, transforming the beams and raw wood floors into more of a cozy home than a storage area over a drafty garage.

"Wow," I said. "Unbelievable."

Jules walked around the small room demonstrating its usefulness. She turned on the TV and showed how they could even play Mario Brothers. She sat down on the floor opposite Brian and Kelli, purposeful and precise, like it was the first time she'd ever sat down in her life. "The only thing we need is a couch."

"How would you get it up here?"

"Easy."

"Well, if you think you can pull it off. Wow," I said again, "this place looks great." I walked around the space admiring their hard work.

I'd been making brownies when Jules called me up, and the mixing bowl of batter was still sitting on the counter with a greased pan next to it. Back in the kitchen I took a spatula and began to pour the batter into the pan, scraping the sides. The oven was already heated up and I slid the pan in and set the timer for thirty minutes. I made brownies two or three times a week, cut them into squares, and put them on a plate on the counter for whoever wandered into the kitchen.

For the next few months, after Jules and Kelli and Brian had dubbed the upstairs room of the garage The Chill Spot, more and more kids started hanging out up there. From the kitchen, I would often watch as two or three of them walked down the driveway. Sometimes they would stop and wave to me through the window. Sweetboy and a handful of guys would skateboard in the driveway, the garage door open where two light bulbs hung from the ceiling, one of them too dim to light much of anything. They moved a quarter pipe to the back of the garage and took turns skating up to the rim, flipping around and back down. Troy, one of Sweetboy's friends, had built a rail with his dad, and they all practiced popping up and sliding along the edge.

One night as I was doing dishes, I saw Troy wipe out. It looked bad so I went outside to make sure he was okay.

It was dusk, that beautiful end of summer gloaming, the sun sunk far behind the trees and past the upper lip of the earth like the day is a soft mouth disappearing. I love that time—the handing off of live things to the mystery of moths seeking light and beetles clicking on screens and windows as though trying to get away from some fearful unknown thing. It was during the gloaming that The Lost Boys usually gathered outside.

Troy slowly stood up. "Shit."

"You alright?" Sweetboy said.

"Yeah, *shit* that hurt."

"Man, dude, your jeans are ripped," Manni, another friend, said.

I went out to take a look. "Are you okay?" He must have hit the driveway in a skid because a deep, bloody scrape was on the side of his knee. Troy and Sweetboy had been friends for years and sometimes we joked around. Once, when he was younger, maybe nine or ten, he'd climbed up on the roof of the breezeway and refused to come down even when I threatened to call his mother. I'd laughed, he'd laughed, I kept threatening, he kept refusing, both of us aware the other wasn't all that serious. Eventually I went back inside and he climbed down.

"You should probably come in and wash it up—come in and I'll wash it up and put bacitracin on it."

"Nah, I'm okay. Thanks, Mrs. James. I'll be okay," and he limped off and sat down on the steps with his one leg straight. As I went back into the kitchen, I thought maybe I should pray for him, so I did. I loved him. I loved all these kids. I didn't want anything to harm them.

* * *

Stamped with *Mickey* and *Snapple* and *Prada* and *Myspace,* in their nebulous glassine bags, heroin is tucked into the wheel wells of cars in slow moving lanes, in the hulls of boats and hulls of airplanes, through tunnels and bolt cut fences—and enters the land of opportunity. They're hated like plastic explosives and loved like favorite uncles. Dealers sneak around corners in silver Hondas with smoked glass windows appearing into scenes and back out, stuffing bills and thumb-sized bags of junk, dope, horse, smack, shot, H, wrapped and stamped to indicate the distributor. They step softly into bedrooms and tuck their children in; all is well and all will be well because I love you to the moon and back. If I should die before I wake, I pray the Lord my soul to take.

RETRIBUTION

WHEN I WAS IN FIFTH GRADE THERE WAS A GIRL, Vicky, who was mentally disabled. Her mother drove her to school. I remember seeing her get out of the back of the station wagon and thinking that her hair looked off kilter, like it had been washed the night before and she'd slept on it wet. I knew her mother always made her sit in the back seat (long before car seats and seat belts) on the way to school so sometimes I imagined her angry and screaming in protest, throwing her head back and forth in some kind of repeated aggression of her head on the seat cushion, so that her hair got clumped and tangled. Her eyes were always a little bit puffy, which seemed to confirm my hypothesis about what happened on her way to school. She sat next to me in class. None of the kids paid much attention to her, me included, even though I knew that the only reason she was different was because of some decision God had made, whatever his reasons.

One day after recess as we were filing in and still out of breath, the room full of the sounds of chairs screeching on the floor and desks being readjusted as the draft of outdoor energy began to die down, I went to a shelf of books lining the wall under the large bank of windows that looked out on the asphalt part of the playground. It was a gray day, probably winter, and I was happy because I'd read through both books that we'd been assigned the previous day. Mrs. Cantell's large oak desk was next to the window, kitty corner to the classroom, and she sat behind it rearranging some papers. There were two shallow bins on her desk, one for completed assignments, and one for graded ones. After sliding the books back into the shelves, I went to the bin for graded assignments and thumbed through looking for a paper I'd already turned in. It hadn't been difficult, and unlike my math assignments, I expected a 100. She looked up and smiled at me. I still hadn't found my paper. "Great job, Katie," she said, which confirmed I had indeed gotten a 100 on it.

I was thrilled because it was obvious this teacher liked me. I wasn't her favorite in the class—I still didn't speak up much—but there was something that made me think she felt like I had potential, or at least that she understood me. I'd been trying hard to pay attention and not look out the windows when she talked, not sketch on my notepaper or write poetry. "Thanks," I said. I was painfully shy.

She pulled the assignment bin over and flipped through the papers until she found mine. There was a large glass jar on her desk filled with marbles. Even though it was bleak outside, the marbles caught the light from the windows and sucked it into their tiny nuclei so that the colors from one bled into another and they became indistinguishable. She handed me two pages stapled together. "I love your description of the horse." The assignment had been to describe in writing a picture of our choice cut from a magazine. The picture we chose was to be pasted on the first page. I had pasted a picture of an Appaloosa, the only type of horse I knew the name of. And then she did what to me seemed the highest honor I could ever hope for as a student. She read one of my sentences back to me. "*The speckles gathered near the tail of the horse and the wheat in the field bended like it was praying.* It's very original that you included the field in your description. And your description of the wheat praying is a wonderful example of metaphor." An example of metaphor was something we were supposed to include in the assignment, but I'd forgotten. I had no idea what a metaphor was.

"Thanks."

She looked up. "Do you think you could write another description from a magazine and perhaps I could put it on the bulletin board?"

"Okay."

She handed me the paper. "Good job, Katie."

"Thanks."

When I returned to my desk, the back of my neck all goosebumpy with encouragement, I pulled my chair out, but when I looked down I saw a tack, needle side up, sitting on the middle of my seat. As I reached down to pick it up Vicky let out something that sounded like a snort. I looked at her and she was covering her mouth trying not to laugh. I held up the tack. She looked at it and started to giggle.

A girl next to me had seen the tack too, and watched as I made my way through the desks to the teacher. I said, "Mrs. Cantell, Vicky put this tack on my chair."

Mrs. Cantell immediately grew serious. Vicky had followed me over and was standing behind me. "Is that true, Vicky?"

She giggled again and nodded. The class began to stir. A boy said, "No way!"

"Did you do it on purpose?"

Vicky held her hand over her mouth and nodded. Then giggled again.

"Katie, were you about to sit on it?"

"Yes," I said.

"Vicky, you can never, ever, do something like that, to hurt someone. You could have really hurt her. Go outside in the hall and wait for me." Mrs. Cantell shook her head and told the class to settle down. She went to talk to Vicky.

I put the thumbtack on my desk and sat down. As I sat there the rest of the class, having found out what happened, began to snicker. My heart sank. I knew I should have tossed the tack in the trash and never mentioned it, except perhaps to Vicky. I know now that she did it because she wanted to be my friend. Vicky's heart was good, and mine was bad. I wanted the class to like me in the same way Vicky wanted me to like her. I still wonder what would have happened if only I'd befriended Vicky.

Left unchecked, our lives can become processions of "if onlys." Like some kind of inverted vision, our "if onlys" will choke out every prayer and verse or hug from a friend. If only I hadn't let Sweetboy stay out late when he was too young. If only I didn't let him use the car that night. Silly. I began to view his first needle as God's retribution for every wrong I'd committed as a parent and back even further, to my sins of long ago, all the way back to when I was a kid myself. Silly.

* * *

One night I woke up to Sweetboy standing next to my bed holding his lit cell phone. It was hard to miss the quaint implications of the light; the glow of it, like it was a candle held aloft in the days of the colonists and Sweetboy was about to tell me to "come quick, Johnny's burning with fever." He nudged my shoulder to wake me up.

"Mom, there's a cop on the back porch. He wants to talk to you."

His voice was trembling ever so slightly. Here is where, in my ever-present commentary on my own commentary of all that took place, I would add a footnote if I was adding footnotes. 1. *Take advantage of the quiver in your son's voice—he's scared, and he should be. For godsake, get angry.*

I heard the word *cop* and immediately looked over at Rick to make sure he'd woken up too. He rose up on an elbow, groggy. "What's going on?"

"I don't know." I climbed out of bed and followed Sweetboy downstairs. The back porch was dark. Sam, who often hung around, was standing next to Max, another friend who sometimes stayed over because he lived farther away. Sam had long stringy hair and an awesome smile that made you like him immediately, and parents trusted him enough to relax whenever he was around, as though a kid with a smile like that could never, by mere constitution, participate in anything untoward. Max was a beautiful boy, tall, with smooth dark skin inherited from an African American father and a Jamaican mother. Sometimes when he was headed to his car he'd shout a quick *bless up* over his shoulder as he left. Sam was wearing a yellow Bob Marley T-shirt, which threatened to render his trustworthy smile null. The shirt glowed yellow in the darkness.

The officer stood next to the boys holding up a small flashlight between his thumb and index fingers like a doctor making sure your pupils contract. He held it up next to his forehead, pointing the light back and forth from Sam to Max and back again. When I came out, he swung the beam of light in my direction and I squinted. Once he realized I was Sweetboy's mother, he let it drop to his side. I could just make out Sam's father walking up the driveway.

"What's going on?" I said, and wrapped my arms around myself to keep warm. I was in sweats and a T-shirt.

Sam's father had a stern look on his face. The officer said, "Is this your son?" and turned on the flashlight again, pointing it in Sam's direction.

"Yes. What's going on?"

"These two boys were riding shopping carts in the back parking lot over at K-Mart. It doesn't look like they've been drinking, and I didn't find any drugs on either of them, but it's after three in the morning. Did you know there's a curfew?" He looked over at me. "Now, they both say that they were sleeping here for the night. Are you aware of this?"

"Yes," I said. "I assumed they were here."

"I apologize," Max said, "I'm sorry about that, Mrs. James."

Sam chimed in too. "Yeah, we're really sorry. We weren't thinking. We won't do it again."

"Yeah, we're really sorry," Max repeated.

I looked at Sweetboy: "Were you with them?"

"No, I was here with Christopher." Christopher is Sam's older brother and he and Sweetboy had become close—he was smart and interesting; he and Rick and Sweetboy would often sit in the living room talking after I went to bed.

"Christopher and me were just hanging out. We just went to bed." It made me cringe to think I was upstairs asleep when all this was going on.

During moments of drama I can become unusually lucid and articulate and fearless. I suppose it's because I don't know what to do except talk. As I looked at the officer and Sam's father and then Max and Sam, who I was responsible for that night. I felt like an idiot. "What were you thinking? You were all the way over at K-Mart?"

"I'm really sorry," Sam said again.

"You guys can't do that. That's just stupid. I thought you were here." I wasn't surprising myself with anything articulate yet. I looked at Sweetboy: "Did you know they weren't here?" I didn't wait for an answer, but instead looked at the officer. "I had no idea they weren't here. I thought they were inside sleeping."

Satisfied that I was aware of the situation and not some gonzo adult smoking pot with the kids, the officer gave one last warning to the boys, turned off the flashlight, and walked back down the driveway. Sam and Christopher's dad put in his two cents, said it was okay for Sam to stay the rest of the night, and left.

"That was really dumb. If you guys stay here, that means we're responsible for you. I need to know where you are. I assumed you were downstairs."

"It won't happen again," Max said.

At that point I took the opportunity to fulfill one of my duties as a parent and tossed them a good wad of lecture. "Respect authority guys. I'm glad you don't do drugs. Or drink (although I wondered if sometimes they did). But you need to respect authority. There will always be authority in your lives, and much that you might not agree with or appreciate (I was on a roll), but you need to get used to it, it will keep you from trouble, give you success. Up in the morning, asleep at night (when they stayed over it wasn't unusual for The Lost Boys to sleep till 1:00 a.m.), your parents want what's best for you." I paused, "But man, if you guys ever do drugs, I swear . . ." Then, as I headed back inside, I said half to myself, "But that flashlight, geeze, I thought he was gonna burn holes in our eyes . . ."

They all broke out laughing.

Here, again, in my commentary of my own commentary, I will say that I was doing okay up until I suddenly sunk to their level and became all laid back about the cop and his flashlight. As bad as my lecture was, it was better than laughing at a cop.

Rick was standing in the kitchen, and when I came inside he said he wanted to go talk to them too but I told him not to bother. I said, "Sam and Max, they were at K-Mart. Sweetboy wasn't with them. Let's talk about it in the morning."

* * *

The Lost Boys had learned the art of dressing in contradictions: to be inspected and to not be inspected. The tie-dyed T-shirts and the never-skinny-jeans; a hatred for anything hipster or preppy; T-shirts that were either plain or with simple snowboard or skater logos, never slogans. No collars. Nondescript, yet descriptive in their very non-descriptiveness. If hoodies were necessary the hoods stayed down. For the most part their jeans didn't sag and their boxers weren't visible. They flattened themselves in the shadows of the world, and yet they wanted to be noticed. Like the hollow wooden notes of a marimba, where each softly pulled hit of the mallet resonates the exact same sound and yet each note is entirely different, The Lost Boys blended with each other in one long percussion of sound that, over and over, beat out a rhythm: *we are.* They grew their hair long, in dreadlocks or curls, and it would momentarily lift off their shoulders as they did ollies in parking lots or next to curbs, cars slowing to pass them. And always, their shoes: Etnies, Vans, Emerica, Fallen. They were noticed, they were not noticed. They skated in circles with their eyes on the pavement.

At first, we often went up to The Chill Spot. Rick would sit down and talk to them about philosophy and God; mini talks, but interesting ones without judgment that he hoped would show them a bigger life, a new way of thinking. They loved Rick; he was funny and interesting and smart and loved them and they felt it. Rick is the most affectionate person I know, and he can make you feel like God himself is placing a hand on your shoulder and saying, "It's okay, I love you and if you're ever interested in talking, I'm here." Frequently, one of the boys would seek

Rick out just to talk. Sometimes they'd come hang out with me in the kitchen and eat brownies. They would talk about how they were doing, what they thought about God. They liked sitting around the kitchen table. I'd made a large painting and hung it over the table—I'd clipped dozens of photos of houses for sale with their asking prices from an Orlando newspaper and pasted them on a huge pegboard, written part of a T. S. Eliot poem between the pictures in charcoal, and covered everything with a thin coat of gesso. The newspaper eventually yellowed. I also drew a crude charcoal sketch of a dove and glued it left of center. I don't know, somehow it all made sense to me.

When I think back on everything, I think The Chill Spot deserves the sort of reverence that The Upper Room does. Proper nouns, both. It was in The Upper Room that Jesus broke the bread, where John leaned on his shoulder, where Judas betrayed him. In The Chill Spot, either mustard seeds were about to sprout, or the jejune fog of adolescence was going to mix with medicants and slam The Lost Boys deaf and dumb. The Evil needed to keep testing the winds and monitoring the temperatures. Infinitesimal sprouts were beginning to show even as The Lost Boys were beginning to poke around in the dubitable fortunes of America: the pills of affluence. In The Upper Room with The Lost Boys. In The Upper Room with The Lost Boys and The Pills.

You stand in the middle of Tiananmen Square with the treads of a tank at your shins but you will stare it down so you stay. The world is watching and they don't know who will win, but you scud back and forth and face it. The tank will run you over. It will crush you bone by bone if you don't get out of its way. There are the words you wrote in chalk on the rafter above your head: "Wake up!" *Fuck "wake up,"* The Evil says, *I'll put you to fucking sleep!* And the plates of the treads creep forward.

The ancient Greek word for workmanship is *poiēma*, the same word for poem in English. *Poiēma* is translated as "workmanship" in the

English Bible, and there's a verse in the Bible that says we are "God's workmanship," which essentially means that we are God's poems. Some poems are long, some are free verse, some sonnets, some haikus. The Bible says God creates lives that are long and short but full of meaning either way. It seems unfair that he creates short lives; those stupid haikus: The grass is so green / The breeze feels cool on my skin / Then I die slowly.

I once knew a woman who died of a rare disease called POEMS. Like flowers, diseases have technical names as well as common names and doctors interchange them both, as much for the people affected as for the ease in pronouncing them. Crow–Fukase syndrome is the technical word for POEMS syndrome, or Takatsuki disease. POEMS stands for polyneuropathy, organomegaly, endocrinopathy, monoclonal gammopathy, and skin changes, which are all features of it. POEMS affects the nerves: numbness, tingling, weakness in the feet. I don't know why the feet. The weakness gets worse until you can't walk. You sweat a lot, you go blind, and then you die.

In *Beautiful Boy*, David Sheff tells the story of his son, Nick, who fell into meth addiction. When Sheff was at an Al-Anon meeting once, someone said that if he didn't believe in God yet, he would.

I don't know if David Sheff believes in God, but I understand what the guy in the Al-Anon meeting meant. I'm too weak not to believe in God. I don't know how atheists can stay sane as they watch their child spiral into a metaphorical abyss—watching a child doing heroin is like watching a slow suicide, like watching them slice their wrists in slow motion, involuntarily pulling out a needle over and over like they're pulling out a knife only to stab themselves again. I can't take the pain / I've failed those I truly love / Maybe I'll die now.

OPIADDICTS

There's no such thing as a fake high. If you're high, you're high, but I'm not sure how else to categorize the things an addict will abuse that don't fit the regular caste of opiates and synthetically produced drugs, such as fentanyl, that are introduced into America's bloodstream via the bellies of airplanes and trucks. They arrive tucked into stuffed animals and behind the panels of cars. Sometimes drugs are stuffed into condoms and for a mere $1,000 a mule will swallow as many as six of them. Their mouths are sprayed with Pill Glide Swallowing Spray to help get them down, and then, bellies bloated, they enter America and shit them out. Heroin is the drug that gets all the attention; another pop-star dies and the media peppers their coverage of it with words like "rash of" and "epidemic." It's almost sexy—and I mean that in the most diabolical of ways.

Imodium, not so much. It's like the opposite of sexy. Some people would find a way to abuse toothpaste if it were possible, and the latest example of this is Imodium. It turns out if you pop enough soft gels or drink enough straight from a bottle, the over the counter, antidiarrheal will get you high. It's undetectable in urine and almost impossible to overdose on.

But you can. Overdose. Essentially, Imodium—its clinical name is loperamide—is an opiate, but because of a protein called P-glycoprotein that pumps it out of the brain, it doesn't make you high. However, if taken in very large quantities, like drinking bottles of the mint-green liquid or swallowing five hundred pills a day, those P-glycoprotein pumps are overwhelmed and stop pumping out the drug so that it builds up in the brain and creates a high. Abusers call the drug "lope."

Once in the brain, Imodium can cause marked depression of the central nervous system as well as heart dysrhythmias that are difficult to correct (CVS, Rite Aid: time to lock up the blue bottles.). One girl with short, cropped hair and beautiful brown eyes, who stayed with us for a short time, began abusing Imodium, overdosed, and suffered permanent heart damage. As far as I know she's doing okay now, but we've lost touch.

So far there haven't been a large amount of overdoses from Imodium, and since it's only recently become better known, doctors are playing catch up. In emergency rooms doctors might test for the usual drugs and find nothing, and yet the heart continues in some kind of vapid decline (the embrocation that the Imodium has stippled around in the brain causes the heart to skip beats, then halt, unable to correct itself, so that the patient needs to be paddled back to life) and it can't seem to get back into the right rhythm; one side powers down or powers up while some white-coated person stands over them ready to administer the next shock. Hopefully the heart will respond and kick back into rhythm, although sometimes it doesn't. There have been a rising number of deaths in the United States due to Imodium abuse, and as it becomes more widespread the assumption is that they will continue to rise. Heroin, however, bypasses the ugly, chalky blue liquid. Heroin overdoses are pretty straightforward.

There's Prince and Michael Jackson and Amy Winehouse and Phillip Seymour Hoffman and Janis Joplin and maybe even Elvis for all we know—as a kid the rumor was that he died on a toilet. I used to picture him slumped over half on the floor, pants still around his ankles. And of course, there are all the other people who've died from overdoses that we will never know, and maybe more important, other people's moms and dads and brothers and sisters and friends and spouses who've watched them die. Oh, and children. The babies without a parent. A child without a parent. The children who live with grandmothers or, almost by accident, wake up one day to find themselves adults after jumping from one foster family to the next.

Sometimes I think about the worst kinds of drugs as enormous shovelfuls of what I know now is a pale, cream colored powder, packed into back alleys and empty lots. In my mind there are usually a handful of pockmarked people; still loved, but intentionally forgotten because it's easier for people who love addicts to forget than to walk around every day with their hearts caved in, loving them so much but not even knowing where they are. If not forgotten, the mind goes to how they were long ago, young and innocent, and this can be the most painful thing of all; thinking about what's been lost. They've become grown children with their mouths open like baby birds. Their necks are stretched ropey and their eyes are bulging with the hunger.

Now, allow me to officially introduce you to the subject at hand: your everyday traditional bag of smack. "Bag" is almost a misnomer. In fact, one hit is tucked into such a tiny bag of glassine paper (it looks like a miniature, folded paper lunch bag the size of a postage stamp) it's hard to distinguish it as a bag. The powder looks almost like residue that's been left in the folds. They're stamped with labels that divulge where they originated from, what dealer or area, *Mickey, 9 Lives, Rocking Horse* . . . and then the more prophetic labels: *Misery, Gotcha, Flatline.* The heroin is emptied into a spoon and then "cooked" via a flame from a lighter. Once it's melted it's sucked into a syringe and the rest is history.

A needle and a bag of heroin is a meteoric run on the brain compared to Imodium's rather slow absorption, but either one can land you in an emergency room in the middle of the night, a doctor leaning over you with the paddles, trying to shock you awake.

And so a guy sits in front of a fluorescent screen: a stalled video game, a movie, it doesn't matter what because he's not paying attention. His arms are mottled with tracks and he has a gray pallor and his veins float above muscle and almost punch through skin as he presses his elbow awkwardly convex. In his other hand he holds a syringe between his thumb and index fingers, his fingers on the flange, his thumb on the orange plunger. As he presses the plunger into the syringe, the heroin eases into the slipstream of blood. The syringe, previously resembling a cross (small t), is flattened into a big T. He nods off while the blue light of the screen keeps on doing whatever it's been doing, whatever it will be doing when he hopefully wakes up.

JEREMIAH

JEREMIAH IS ITALIAN with dark hair and the bluest eyes I've ever seen. When he was a Lost Boy he had dreads that he kept telling us, as though embarrassed by them, he planned to cut off. He taught me how to make lasagna the way his mother did, with real ricotta cheese, not cottage cheese and precooked noodles the way I'd always made it. When he first started coming over he was going to college at Temple and doing a decent amount of drugs, more of the weed, hallucinogen type, probably a molly here and there, maybe coke, but I doubt he would ever have tried heroin. That said, the acid had messed his brain up a bit and conversations sometimes got as tangled and cragged as his dreadlocks. I would sit at the table with him and try to steer the conversation into some kind of cognitive sense. Rick and I quickly grew to love him.

One night I sat with him in the kitchen, the window behind him dark except for a reflection from a light that hung low over the table. Both of us were carving designs into Jenga blocks. Someone had already carved "Piper" into mine, and I was filling in the other side, scratching repeating triangles into the wood with a pen. Piper was a girl who came over from time to time. Once, she and Jules spent an evening making Christmas ornaments out of felt, and often our dining room table was cluttered with drawing pads and markers and paints, a few kids at work on something, especially when Jules and Sophie were still at home. Sometimes I gave impromptu art lessons in a studio I have upstairs in the open space next to our bedroom. I would together a still life—usually a piece of fruit next to a silver plated dish of some kind so that there was a complicated reflection of the fruit on the silver—and a few easels and guide a couple kids through the basics of painting. Some were surprisingly talented. The ones who weren't usually stood back from their work and laughed.

That night Jeremiah was wearing a drug rug, one of those sweater-like shirts made of hemp with ties at the neck that look like they'd give you a rash if you slept in one. There's a lot of names for them: hookah hoodie, joint jacket, cannabis coat. . . . He was easy to talk to, and I always enjoyed being with him, talking one-on-one. As he worked at scoring lines into his block, he told me he was done with drugs and every once in a while he'd look up and his blue eyes made me feel like I could stare right through them to every acid trip he'd ever taken. Drug rug notwithstanding, as he talked, I was surprised. I'd always thought of him as not so interested in drugs. More of a drinker. I had no idea he was into acid. By that time his mother and I had gotten together for coffee and a few walks, talking about Jeremiah and Sweetboy and then praying for them. When he told me he was done with drugs I told him I was so glad and it was the best decision he'd ever made, and then asked him why he all of a sudden decided not to do them anymore. He told me about a dream he'd had, or vision—he wasn't sure which. His mother was the charismatic type of Christian, speaking in tongues and things like that, so the fact that a dream or vision was in the mix didn't surprise me. It seems to me that charismatic Christians are especially sensitive to spiritual things.

"I was in some kind of darkness where nothing made sense and it just made me depressed, like I was really depressed." At that point it was hard to tell if he was talking about real life or his dream. "It was all the drugs. There were words and the words were all over the place and they just kept coming, I would see them, one and then another, and I felt closed in." He was talking slowly but he smiled from time to time as he turned a Jenga block around in his hands. The block had an arrow carved into one side, the kind of arrow that has lines pointed out at the ends that indicate feathers the way they're drawn on chalkboards for weddings, on farm tables next to cupcakes.

As we talked, a boy with long hair that was dyed bright orange came in the kitchen and headed into the basement looking for Sweetboy. I'd seen him before. Always hanging back, silent in the background. I never learned his name. He would come and go, his orange hair making a kind of moving bull's eye surrounded by the other kids. He would float around the house like a fishing bobber, disappear for days and then show up again. He said hi before heading to the basement.

"It wasn't like a dream, it was more a vision, something like that," Jeremiah continued, "and then there were words that didn't make any sense, and I saw all these words that were really dark, like *death* and *empty*, and I knew they were part of drugs, that the words are what would happen if I kept doing them, that I would be empty and depressed, like if I kept using them they'd make me crazy, so I was depressed."

"In the dream you were depressed, or in real life?"

"I guess so. Yeah." He grabbed a handful of blocks and began setting them one on top of another until they were about to fall. "It was messing with my brain, all the drugs and the darkness. I know it was God that gave me the vision, the Holy Spirit. After all the darkness and drugs and depression, as clear as, I don't know, really clear words just came in front of everything else and they were light and I could tell I didn't feel depressed anymore and that I didn't have to choose darkness anymore. It's like I knew I had a choice. I was doing a lot of drugs. Then the words *Choose Life* showed up. They were big. And I knew as soon as I saw them that I had been given a choice and that if I waited any longer I wouldn't have a choice anymore. So I chose life."

"Wow, Jeremiah."

"So yeah, I'm done with them. Yeah."

After that night Jeremiah did change. He went through a couple stages where he tried to figure out God and ended up with a few crazy ideas, but overall, slowly, we could tell something was different in him. I don't know if he abruptly stopped using drugs because of his vision or if he had some starts and stops—I know it wasn't an easy time for him. But as time went on, we could see his mind beginning to clear, becoming more lucid. Eventually he decided to go on a missions trip to work in the slums of Indonesia, and that's when he started reading his Bible.

Rick began having a Bible study every Wednesday night. In the winter everyone sat around the fireplace and talked. There were only a few kids at first, but after a couple months the room was full; kids would squish onto the couch and sit on the floor as the fire blazed. Jeremiah fed it logs until it reached up to the flue and crackled and popped out a tiny ember onto the Persian carpet from time to time because we didn't use a screen. Most were around seventeen through twenty-five, and completely different. They didn't all do drugs. Some grew up in stable families that went to church every Sunday, and even as they grew older and moved on, kept going to church and kept reading their Bibles and kept growing in their faith. Others still went to church but weren't sure they believed anything they'd learned when they were growing up. Some were using drugs and didn't care about much of anything and I had no idea why they came. Others were doing drugs and wanted to stop. (More than a few times one boy in particular, tall and thin, almost lanky, came and sat to the right of the fire where he leaned against the wall and kept nodding off even as everyone talked. I truly believe The Lost Boy nodding off was coming because he desperately wanted to stop doing drugs and thought maybe coming to our house would magically make it happen. He had been in Sophie's fourth grade class and I remember him at an end of the year pool party bursting up through the water and flipping his hair with a sideways half-shake of his head, laughing, and then diving under again. During the Bible study I would watch as his shoulders gave way to the slow travel of sleep until his head hung down over his chest. The fire must have overheated one whole side of him. I found myself with a strange maternal desire to lift him up and carry him to bed.)

Some were in recovery. Some came because their parents made them come, dropping them off at our front door. At first I went to the Bible study too and sat next to Rick and tried to be like Socrates and ask brilliant rhetorical questions, but eventually it seemed better for me to stay upstairs and pray as I listened to the muffled voices and silences and sometimes sudden bursts of laughter I heard coming up the stairs from the living room.

Sweetboy was usually in the living room too, but then he'd go grab a smoke and wouldn't come back. For me, that was the hardest part—that Rick was hanging out with everyone, but his own son seemed to care less. When I was downstairs, if I saw Sweetboy leave, my heart would sink and everyone talking around me would fade so that, like a dog attentive to a certain sound becomes deaf to the rest of the world, the voices in the room became nothing but white noise to me. I was selfish that way, all I wanted was for Sweetboy to come back. Sometimes I'm not sure how much I even cared about The Lost Boys.

Eventually the study petered out, although a handful of kids kept coming over to talk. That's when Christopher really started hanging around. He wasn't very talkative, and would often leave with Sweetboy to grab a cigarette, but he always came back in. He slept over a lot and eventually I made up a bed in the basement for him and he moved in. He was the oldest of Sweetboy's friends. He was a soccer star in high school and was an Eagle Scout. Every parent's dream kid. I felt somehow proud of him. He and Sweetboy would talk late into the night—on the porch with their cigarettes then down in the basement and then back up, a pattern that repeated itself until they finally fell asleep—about life and truth and God. Every once and a while Rick hung out with them until two or three in the morning because they had fallen into some intellectual rabbit hole and needed a little help to find their way back. I think sometimes the three of them even prayed together. Sometimes I'd wake up around three or four in the morning and hear them downstairs talking.

Eventually I found out that Sweetboy, Christopher, and Christopher's younger brother, Sam, would occasionally drive out to a park with a couple six packs and talk or mess around. Sometimes other Lost Boys went too. Sweetboy told me that one night they went to a small farm I often passed on my way to the grocery store. It's the kind of place kids go to for summer camp and has goats and a large tepee and a handful of old wood play sets. In a small fenced in area there are usually a few goats on top of a wooden shelter sliding their jaws sideways as they chew their food. There's also a Shetland pony. The night Sweetboy and a few of The Lost Boys went to the farm, they coaxed the pony out of the gate and led it across the road to a small Cape Cod with a fenced in backyard and left it there. I laughed when he told me about it.

I thought about all of this the night Sweetboy left. I'm not sure why it stayed with me, perhaps because it's the way I always thought things should be—harmless and funny like a high school prank. Something they'd be laughing about for years.

I once saw a picture of Sweetboy on Facebook sitting in a stuffed chair in the middle of the night next to overgrown bushes with a beer in one hand, the flash from the camera, like a fluorescent explosion, having for one infinitesimal moment appeared and then disappeared, leaving his face chalk white. He was wearing a tie-dyed T-shirt and a hat and was smiling.

SKIN HEADS

IT WAS LIKE an ambush of Marlboro reds in the breezeway. Obviously, they couldn't do drugs in the breezeway and in The Chill Spot we checked on them, so they smoked cigarettes—first American Spirits (which I was told, and didn't believe, weren't habit forming because they didn't have additives), packaged in a cool looking blue box with colorful feathers that made them look deceptively organic—a nod to both the Grateful Dead as well as Native Americans and peace pipes—point being, they were natural and possibly even good for you. (There's a widely held belief that natural equals healthy and it drives me crazy: opium is natural, coca leaves are natural, snake venom is natural.) So the kids smoked their "natural" cigarettes convinced they'd never smoke a "real" cigarette. It was a matter of months before the empty garden pot, a stand-in for an ashtray, was filled with the smashed stubs of Marlboros.

Smoke followed them around like the dust of horses.

* * *

Max, the boy Sam was with the night he rode the shopping carts in the K-Mart parking lot, is a gifted artist and he seemed to like the art, the sketches and paintings in our home, and the way people would often be sitting at the dining room table drawing or doodling or stitching something together. He lived forty minutes away, so when he came over he tended to stay for a while. At one point, his mother called—she wanted to make sure we were here and that it was a safe place for him to be. I told her we kept tabs on things and that there wasn't any drinking or drugs. I told her a lot of them smoked but that was about it. Some of Max's art was simple cartoon drawings of people, almost childlike, that captured something unique about them. They were funny but also somehow profound. He drew Sweetboy on the couch in The Chill Spot playing Mario Brothers. Sweetboy was leaning back with his head resting on a cushion; the emphasis was on his hair and his hands. His hair flopped over one eye and his hands were too large and covered the console like the paws of a lion.

There's an abandoned house called The Cult House about thirty minutes from here where kids sometimes go at night. I've seen a picture of it and it's covered with vines that have grown up and over the roof and through windows hollowed out like empty eye sockets. It's one of those places, like watching *The Exorcist* on TV, that pulls fear from the ground and the wood of the house and the hovering atmosphere around it so that it feels like it will swallow you up if you're not aware of the fact that it's real like an exorcism is real, like The Evil is laughing from behind a tree somewhere and you need to be careful. Sometimes brave kids go inside the house and look around.

The road that leads to the house is called Devil's Road and is lined with trees (Sweetboy showed me a picture of it on his phone) but the trees, instead of arching over the road the way they usually do—like a line of soldiers touching swords above a bride and groom—instead arch outward as though yanked back by their leaves like a line of helpless women with their hair caught in someone's fists. When Sweetboy showed me the picture, the road looked like an enormous zipper split open by mysterious air. Then he told me what happened the night he and The Lost Boys tried to find The Cult House.

The moon is a sweet friend if you're on the back porch looking up, but an accomplice to fear if you're on some lonely dark road out in the middle of nowhere; the area is legendary and fear doesn't skim the ground like it can easily be outrun. There are a few YouTube videos of the road filmed from the dashboards of cars, and even though you only see headlights shining on a dark road with creepy trees on either side, it looks like you're about to encounter a Delphinianly dark personality. The Evil on that road could plunder a soul.

The road curves here and there and there are a few hills. That night Christopher was driving, Sweetboy was in the passenger seat, and Max and Sam were in the back seat. The windows were rolled down, and they were all smoking when a truck approached from behind, tailgated them, and started flashing its lights. It pulled up closer, bumper to bumper, and turned on a floodlight so that the back seat of their car was flooded with light. Max turned around to look and the truck suddenly swerved and pulled up beside them—a guy began yelling out the window.

The truck swerved away, swerved back, and then hit the car, swiping a dent along the side as though trying to drive them off the road. The guy kept yelling eff this and effing that, *n----r* then held up a white hood, smiled, and began throwing rocks at the car. He lifted the hood up again and gave them the finger. Sweetboy told Max to duck, turned around, and pushed his head down on the seat. More effing this and effing that and *N* this and effing *N* all while trying again and again to drive them off the road. Christopher made a hard left, skid a U-turn, headed the other way, and hit the gas but the truck did the same, pulling back up to their bumper. They followed them for miles, all the way back into town until the traffic made their pursuit impossible and the truck finally turned around.

Sometimes I think The Evil is like a virus in so many forms. It gets into the blood and stays latent until circumstances are optimal, then blasts up and out like a car bomb in Syria.

DREAMS

IN THE WEST, we don't take our dreams very seriously. We laugh about how we woke up right when the neighbor from down the street was telling us that he and his cat had made a Sweet Lady of Imperial Perfection cake for us. But that's about it. By the end of the day it's forgotten.

I don't think there's always some deeper meaning behind our dreams, but I've come to believe that sometimes there is, that sometimes a Sweet Lady of Imperial Perfection cake is worth a second glance.

In the Middle East dreams are considered messages from God. The culture's emphasis on dreams causes them to pause and turn a dream around in their mind's eye and deconstruct whatever oddness they're waking from until the meaning becomes clear. In most Middle Eastern cultures dreams aren't ignored but held tight like precious stones.

I've been told writers are allowed two dreams in a book of fiction. But since this is a book of nonfiction, I'll take liberties. Most dreams are fascinating for the dreamer but as boring as a can of soup for whomever has to listen to them. Dreams with visions tucked in them on the other hand, pop up out of the ethereal world beyond and startle you.

By the time The Lost Boys began smoking American Spirits and then Marlboros in our backyard I had started to pray more. I prayed for Sophie and Jules and Sweetboy and The Lost Boys. At that time I didn't know the extent that kids had begun messing with bottles of painkillers from parents' and grandparents' medicine cabinets, but I wasn't an idiot when it came to garden variety drugs. We weren't yet at the point of testing Sweetboy or telling anyone to stop coming over, but we knew the danger was there. Drinking, weed (I was constantly sniffing for the soury smell of it and looking out for red, glassy eyes or ravenous hunger that emptied our pantry or bursts of laughter that seemed too giggly for their ages). I didn't know yet about the telltale pin-dot pupils that accompany a brain full of opiates.

It was when I began praying more—in earnest—that I began having dreams. Or visions. I'll call them visions because I always had them while I was praying and in that half state of sleep, when you're waking up or falling asleep, half here, half there. The meanings of the visions were always clearly responses to prayer and went hand in hand with promises. Although I didn't know it yet, I was beginning to watch my son die. He was getting sucked into the vortex of drugs, deeper than I could have ever imagined—and even though I didn't understand how deep he was, I could still feel him slipping away.

About a year after The Lost Boys began hanging out here, Jules left for California without a return ticket home. Initially, she'd gone to San Francisco for an internship, but when she returned home, she decided she wanted to go back to live there. She was seventeen and hadn't graduated from high school. She worked at Blockbuster until she had enough money for her ticket, and flew back. She finished high school online. Inherited fortune notwithstanding, in our minds she perfectly fit the story of the prodigal son, so I was praying for her a lot.

* * *

Jules and the flowering bush: One morning, as I was praying and still in the shade-light of half sleep, I saw a large, green bush and I knew it was Jules. The bush was flourishing, and as I watched, it began to flower— the most beautiful light green, almost white, flowers I had ever seen. It was covered with them, and as I looked, my heart soared with joy and love for God, and thankfulness. I knew God was telling me he was answering my prayers and that Jules, just like the flowers on the bush, would keep growing. I thanked him as I looked at the flowers, over and over, just as I had prayed over and over *please God, please God,* I prayed *thank you God, thank you God.* But then, as I was thanking him, the bush became dark green again and the flowers disappeared as quickly as they had appeared. My heart sank. My God, my Lord in Heaven, *why?* But then, in the middle of my distress, I looked closer, and realized there never had been flowers. What had looked like flowers had actually been the light green of new growth. O Jules, O Alnilam, my second star. "Like a tree planted by streams of water." Thank you my God and my King.

* * *

On a country road with a country bird: This time I was walking on a narrow country road on a summer day and there were trees on both sides of the road, not tall trees, almost hedges, but high enough to line the road with green and provide some shade. I could glimpse between them what looked like fields of wheat. It was very sunny but I wasn't hot. As I walked, about four feet in front of me, slightly to my left at eye level, a yellow bird flew, slowly, almost hovering, and it looked back at me from time to time to make sure I was still following it. As I followed my feet barely touched the ground, I was so happy. The road stretched out in front of me and I was happy. The bird's name was Providence and I was chosen to follow of my own accord.

PART
TWO

STEPHAN

It was evening, two weeks after Christmas, when Stephan showed up with a ragged copy of David Brainerd's diary.

I was sitting on the couch facing the front window where the Christmas tree had been. Rick was sitting across from me working on his laptop, the glow of the small apple from his Mac a stand-in for the lower part of his face. I was reading a book and through the window the neighbors' Christmas lights were blinking in my periphery when Jack, a boy Jules had dated in high school, brought Stephan in from the kitchen. "This is Stephan. I used to do drugs with him," he said, and left to go hang out with the other Lost Boys.

There was the warmth of the fire and the two large charcoal nudes over the mantel that I've since taken down. I'd just added another log to the fire and was reading *White Noise* for the third time. I was at the part where one of the characters, a kid named Heinrich, is looking out the upstairs window of his bedroom with binoculars for a toxic cloud headed for his family's home.

Stephan sat down in one of the chairs. He was thin, not particularly tall, and blond in the way that you understand it will never fade; when he's fifty he'll still be blond. The tips of his eyelashes matched his hair and he was wearing black pants. I could hear The Lost Boys in the kitchen laughing. Something hit a wall, probably one of the tangerines I usually kept in a bowl on the table that they often messed around with, trying to juggle or score points by tossing them in the bowl. I flexed the spine of my book and placed it upside-down on my lap.

Stephan was silent at first but I realized right away he wasn't a shy kid. It seemed like he was being silent for some intentional reason and it somehow bothered me.

Rick closed his computer halfway, looked at him, and said, "I know you from somewhere."

"It's because you know my dad." I could tell he was used to saying this.

"No way," Rick said. "Wait, you're Brad Meenan's son!" (It still amazes me that he immediately knew who Stephan's father was.) "He's president of Mercy Global Missions, right? I haven't seen him for a long time . . ."

A pause. "We look exactly alike," Stephan said. I would eventually learn that his intermittent silences were sometimes for good and sometimes for bad and always hard to figure out. He was rolling the thin paperback in his hands, kneading it into a stocky tube of newsprint. His hands were pale, with a few random freckles.

He seemed serious, and young, and even though he looked healthy, I could tell he'd skimmed past youth, skipped vital stages of growth, and been on the verge of falling in among the huddle of the quickly aged—that place where homeless people on sidewalks seem born into, like there was no birth; they were never infants who needed to be fed or changed, or were held gently as someone lifted a bottle to their mouth. Every once and a while if I see an old and weathered person on the street with one eyelid permanently stuck closed or lips so thin it's hard to imagine them ever having eaten, I'll try to think of them as babies; the water-smooth skin and the way of moving that babies have—in jerks and starts like they know the beginning of a movement but not the end—laughing at goofy faces in front of them, the happiness in others, smiling at the sight of another smile. I wonder about the drug addicts on the street and try to grasp who they were years ago and it bothers me that I can't. Heroin is like an oily chain with a gear of addiction that finally catches and circles around, each revolution a tighter turn of sorrow. There's an unfortunate hope that the gear will keep holding you, even as sorrow increases with each rotation like a penny circling the rim of a large bowl, lower and lower, like it's about to drop but it never does. The penny came from someplace, but once it starts to circle the rim it doesn't matter where.

"You're Rick James," Stephan said. Long pause. "My dad told me about you."

"We met when he spoke at a church I was at. He's great." Rick, enthusiastic, encouraging as always. "You look exactly like him . . ."

"You probably met my mom too."

"Wait," I said, "did I meet him?" I looked at Rick. I kept combing my mind and came up with nothing.

"You wrote a book," Stephan said. "My dad's teaching it for one of his classes." Rick had written a book about Christianity a few years prior. "He said he wanted to have you visit the class and that he really respected you." A quick smile crossed his face.

"That's why you came here?" I said.

"No"—short pause this time. "Jack said I should meet you. He found out I wasn't doing drugs anymore. I didn't know you were the Rick James who wrote the book until now."

"So you guys did drugs together?" Rick said, "You and Jack?"

Stephan nodded. "Yessss . . . it's been three weeks." Another silence. "Three weeks ago I got scared and decided I should stop. I went to Tennessee to see my parents for Christmas and just stopped using. I stopped smoking cigarettes too. All I do now is pray and read . . . this," he indicated the book in his hand, "and the Bible."

* * *

Addicts are rattled by either more drugs or sobriety. Always one or the other, never in between except for what I imagine might be a necessary imperceptible millisecond during the shift from one state to the other; feeling like they'll die if they stop using and knowing they'll die if they keep using. But sober people have the power to choose. Not as easy for someone with a needle in one hand.

Stephan was from a missionary home and that made his sit-down-and-spend-time-with-us-like-a-good-kid more marked. He was good at it. But I knew right away he sincerely wanted to remain sober and that evening—with the fire going and Rick on his laptop and me paused in *White Noise* where Heinrich is looking out the window and Stephan with his deformed book in his hands—we came to trust him and he came to trust us. At that point we were stupid about addicts. We weren't the kind of stupid that gives them money, or assumes once an addict stops he'll never start using again, but still we were stupid. Stephan was too, but we trusted each other as though that night we had made a pact that couldn't be broken.

"Brainerd's great," Rick said, "he, like, gets tuberculosis and keeps going around preaching to the Indians. He sleeps on the ground in the middle of winter, coughs up half a lung, and then gets back on his horse to go around and preach."

"He gets the *consumption*," I said. I had just finished *Angela's Ashes* before I picked up *White Noise* and was having a hard time kicking the Limerick vernacular. My mind was deep in books. *My brothers are dead and my sisters are dead and Jesus, Mary, and Joseph, let's go to the pub and get a pint.*

Stephan nodded slowly. "Yeah, Brainerd's great . . . I just keep reading it. And praying."

"Was it hard," Rick asked, "to quit?"

"Not really. Well, yeah." He laughed a little. "It was *so* hard."

* * *

The thing to know about opiates is that they make you *feel* love and make you *feel* like you love others. Fake love, both. Once they're in your blood the shuck and jive love seeps around and into the empty corners of yourself. You could be standing next to Hitler himself and with even just a few crushed and sniffed oxys, that patch of mustache isn't so repulsive, it's actually kind of endearing. And for the record, no, I've never abused pain pills. But I'm a keen observer, and most addicts not only don't mind talking about their drug of choice, they usually *want* to talk about it.

One night I asked a couple of The Lost Boys to paint our upstairs floors white so that my studio would reflect light and feel more spacious. After they painted them I liked to sit up there while the boys were downstairs tossing tangerines around and sketch and paint and read.

* * *

Stephan needed a place to stay that was far from his old friends who used, and so that very night when Jack brought him into our living room with the roaring fire and the frost slowly eviscerating the window-panes so that the neighbors' lights were foggy in my periphery, we told him he could live with us. *Of course you can*, we said. We had an extra room and it wasn't for nothing he'd shown up right after getting his life together and needed a place to stay and that Rick knew his father. Rick looked at me and I nodded, or perhaps just smiled the tiniest bit. And so it was, Stephan would move into Sophie's room since she was still away at college. The next day he carted in boxes of stuff that included pictures of his family, clothes, more shoes than a teenage boy should ever own, a boogie board (I later learned he had stolen it), and an oscillating fan (again, stolen).

Again, although prone to weighty silences, Stephan wasn't shy, and we soon learned his story, which seemed to me an accumulation of grace upon grace; the first grace being the grace of God (or as C. S. Lewis calls it, severe grace, or severe mercy) that showed him that he clearly needed help, the second grace being the help. These things usually aren't apparent until remembered from the vantage point of looking back. I know we're all given grace if we ask for it and it can come in many ways, often invisible, but for Stephan—so recently saved by it—it was barely in the past at all—the grace was tangible, brick and mortar de facto. It showed up in the form of a real bush he could have reached out and touched, almost like Moses in the desert where the shrub burned prophetic, only Stephan's real bush, and then real bird and real sky, burned their messages silently into his heart. At first he didn't know the beauty of these things even though he was walking outside in the midst of them. The bush was lush and of the normal sort and had berries but it wasn't on fire.

He began using drugs the way most kids do, cigarettes in an alley next to school, then drinking, then weed, and so forth. Once kids get addicted to Marlboros they begin hanging out in clusters of like-mindeds practicing smoke rings and enjoying some kind of brotherly love for the person across from them, all breathing in the same soft calm of maternal smoke. I think of nicotine in the lungs as a mother and heroin as a father; nicotine's always there with the comfort, *Oh sweetheart, it's okay, you'll feel better soon,* and heroin is the stuff of fathers, *You need me far more than you realize.* Sometime in middle school Stephan began dogging around with a posse of kids with the same malformed invincibility that he had. He told me that's how it was— they thought nothing would ever own them, they were the ones who chose what they did or didn't do, not human authority, and certainly not whatever hyped-up authority drugs supposedly had.

That's when he started hanging out with Waylen. They hung Marlboros from the insides of their lips and practiced smoke rings. They stood in their klatch of friends with the smoke rings and then joints and roaches and whatever bongs look like now, then pills, then coke and crack and mollies and ecstasy, then heroin.

Waylen was big and so was his heart. He was loyal. As hollowed out as his insides might have been, he would never leave a friend who needed him. He protected those he loved. One time, when he was in his early 20s, long after the cluster of smokers in the hypothetical alley next to school had thinned out—those with the good sense to leave having left—and then swelled again with new kids who had gotten a taste of milk and honey and wanted more, Waylen, who by that time was dealing, went into the city with a few other guys because they'd made contact with some Colombians who said they'd sell them drugs. And here is where I will take you on a little field trip to The Badlands because like a golden decoy, it's a magnet for an addict.

There's a set of tracks that snake through Philadelphia. One section travels north and south through The Badlands, which is a short walk from the intersection of Kensington Avenue and Somerset Street. The tracks are on a raised mound of gravel and dirt that slopes down on either side into a wooded gully. It's leafy in the summer, which would be almost bucolic if it weren't for the riot of detritus nestled under and behind branches and leaves. Scattered under the canopy of green are ubiquitous white plastic bags from CVS or Target, or gray ones from Walmart. The occasional generic one with a *thank you* and a smiley face under it. There's cardboard and particle board leaning against trees with plastic tarps and blankets covering them for privacy. And mattresses. Folded in half, greasy, ripped, sometimes clean looking, sometimes leaking stuffing. Posturepedic, Serta, Sealy, extra firm, memory foam, box springs, and pillow tops. There are the clothes. Shoes and jeans and shirts. And as though flung from an enormous and generous hand in the sky like seed on a bare lawn, needles. The needles are telltale with their bright orange caps tossed aside and littering the ground indicating that one more plastic syringe, like a whip hand, had snapped one more addict asleep. The people come from everywhere; they are sons and daughters and neighbors and were nursed by bottle or breast. They come from the city and they come from the suburbs, but none of them want to be there. They've learned another language: "Mollies" and "Xanies" and "Subs." The National Geographic Channel called The Badlands "one of the largest open-air drug markets in the eastern United States."

* * *

Usually, those living in The Badlands are happy to sit with you and talk. They will freely tell you where they come from and when and how they began using heroin. Sometimes they'll shoot up as they talk so you try not to stare while they press a needle into their arm or leg or neck (done by someone else because it's hard to get a needle into your neck). They'll talk of the good homes they left and the way they've hurt families. The shame seems to run deep and I wonder if talking about the shame itself has a way of relieving it—of thinking it might keep others from trying heroin—warning people how quickly it will take over your life and then you'll lose the love you used to know, seeking absolution. They are human, gifted, beautiful, and loved by God.

The Badlands, although full of every drug imaginable, is mostly full of heroin. It's a carnival of opiates. On the corners of Kensington and Somerset, dealers yell out *dope, mud, snowball, skag, horse*, like the occasional street preacher with his bullhorn yelling what they've probably already heard about Jesus and forgiveness and love. Sometimes I imagine famous people living in the Badlands because of course even famous people can end up there. Even people who seem to have it together, like Oprah Winfrey or Dan Rather. What about Dr. Oz? What about Elon Musk? What if Elon Musk broke his arm at 17, was given a bottle full of Oxycodone, took more than he should have to ease the pain, then more, and more, then ended up on the needle? I'm sure any number of people in their makeshift homes in the ditches on the side of the tracks could have been a journalist, or a senator, or a famous heart surgeon if they'd never had that first pill.

When Stephan told me about Waylen and the Colombians, I pictured them in a dark room in a basement with red walls and a black ceiling, a heavy velvet curtain for a door, standing in front of Pablo Escobar himself.

As soon as Waylen and his friends got there, things began to unravel quickly because so and so or this guy or that guy hadn't paid enough, or the drugs were cut with baking soda or there weren't enough bags or the dealers were just plain in a bad mood or whatever makes people like that angry, because the Colombians threatened them and then pulled out guns and Waylen basically said don't you effing touch my friends, at which point someone pointed a gun at Waylen's face. This was going to be it; Waylen would die protecting his friends. Instead, he was pistol-whipped so hard his jaw broke and he had to have it wired shut. He told his parents he tripped and fell.

Waylen and Stephan eventually became best friends. They lived across the street from one another and sometimes Waylen went over to Stephan's for dinner. Stephan's family was in the habit of going around the table and sharing what the best part of their day was. When it was Waylen's turn he would get rattled, so eventually, before he went over for dinner, he started writing out the best part of his day on a scrap of paper so he'd be prepared. I don't know if he stopped coming over once he and Stephan started doing hard drugs. Stephan grew up in a family that shared the best part of their days during dinner and yet he still ended up on heroin. It's complicated. Drugs travel through labyrinthine pathways to reach their tribes.

Stephan told me that he and Waylen tried a new drug every time they had a birthday, like an annual holy sacrament. When Stephan's seventeenth birthday was coming up they planned to finally try heroin. But Stephan was having a hard time waiting for his birthday, and so when he was hanging out with some of his most baked friends he tried it with them and not with Waylen. Waylen was hurt that he hadn't waited for him. Even though Stephan left that world long ago he still feels bad that he didn't wait for Waylen before he tried heroin for the first time.

By the time Stephan's parents moved to Tennessee he had ethered himself cadaverous, and even though they knew he was doing drugs, they didn't realize to what extent. Stephan stayed in the Philly area with friends. I assume his accommodations included access to whatever he wanted on the kitchen table every morning like the way a mother might set out cereal. Maybe a couple bags of smack next to a dirty plate. Lay a few fives down, take the day's requirement to feed the habit, and you're all set. By that time he must have felt homeless even if he had a roof over his head.

As Stephan tells it, the night things began to change he was headed somewhere to buy heroin in his faded gold Pontiac littered with empty packs of Marlboro Lights and ash from cigarettes—the upholstery on the door was riddled with burn marks—and suddenly realized that he no longer had a choice; he had to get dope or he felt like he would die. He'd always assumed he had the willpower to stop whenever he wanted, so he'd kept using. He wasn't the same as those people who end up sleeping in makeshift tents next to train tracks. He was different. He could always quit.

That night, on his way to get heroin, he still felt invincible, convinced he could stop whenever he wanted to. It was cold out. Almost Christmas. His family was in Tennessee and the road was disappearing under his tires like staccato lines of yellow coke. There's an itch that starts climbing up your arms and legs and then your torso when your body begins to crave more heroin, and it had already begun. He hadn't shot up since that morning. Dendritical wires in his head were splitting and crossing and curling into sharp pockets of confusion, and whatever it was that had been keeping him lucid was draining so fast he began grinding his teeth and drove even faster. But then, like a car that quickly shifts from fifth gear to first, he suddenly realized he couldn't stop and that no matter what, he had to get heroin. Even if he wanted to, he wouldn't be able to turn his car around. He was unable to. His car was like a phenomenon of his conscious state that had meshed so completely with his unconscious they were barely discernible. He would quit at Christmas. In Tennessee. He had to. That was the plan.

When he got to Tennessee he sat in a recliner in the living room with a blanket, shaking and sweating and cold. He was wan and thin. When he moved in with us he showed me a picture of himself in Tennessee with his family. He was standing next to his dad smiling but his eyes were sunken and gray. By then his parents knew how sick he was, but they didn't say anything, they just hugged him and welcomed him home. He told me when he first got there, he'd hugged his father and whispered in his ear, "Help me."

He stayed in the chair for two weeks as people came and went. He made trips to the bathroom and experienced sudden uncontrollable jerks, but he stayed there, wrapped up in a blanket, until the worst was over.

When you detox your poop runs yellow and you vomit until your teeth feel like horse's teeth, large and immovable even as your lips curl into themselves and the pain hits every nerve in your body. Before Stephan told us these things, they were foreign to us. The closest I'd come to understanding the un-virtues of heroin and its aftermath was when I'd read about "kicking the habit" in the book *Run Nicki Run* as a kid. Eventually Rick and I would see firsthand what "kick the habit" looked like as we watched Sweetboy in a hospital bed, legs startling uncontrollably as heroin left his body like he was trying to kick it away.

Stephan's parents' small house was on a farm and the fields were expansive. There were horses and cows and split rail fences that if seen from miles above the earth would have looked like stitches from a needle, the rails like thread between each plunge of fence post.

When he was able to think clearly again, Stephan began walking outside. He could see the horizon beyond the fields and the glow of a disappearing sun as it tugged the last light from the land.

He remembers when he began to see. It was as if his eyes had been opened after so many years of haze, and like the blind man's eyes that Jesus twice rubbed spit and mud into before the man could see, Stephan discovered that the fog of green earth that had for so many years been pushed aside was beautiful. As he walked outside he saw the sky and the fields and the trees in a new way, as though he was a child again, and when he was passing a bush he stopped and looked at it for a long time as though he'd never seen a bush before. It was magnificent, and he began to feel like some dark subbituminous coal within him was beginning to glow again. The sky became true, and grass, and birds, and his family—people. At that moment Stephan was waking up. His life would be filled with starts and stops and dips and climbs, but there was no doubt that the spirit of God had settled gracious upon him. I wanted that so much for Sweetboy. I wanted *him* to see the sky and fields and trees and bushes.

* * *

One night after Stephan moved in, I came into his room and found him lying prone on the floor. A Bible was open next to him and when he realized I was there he stood up. There were tears in his eyes that he quickly wiped away. The first few months after he moved in, he sat in our living room with a chair pulled up to the fire and read the Bible. He listened to a contemporary Christian song, *Oh, How He Loves You and Me* over and over on his laptop until Rick and I were about to pull our hair out. In the Bible St. Paul tells Timothy to fan to flame the gift that is in him. I guess that's what Stephan was doing.

GUNS AND ARROWS

PEOPLE ESCAPING HEAVY DRUGS can have a particular affinity for angels, for supernatural *goodness*. Maybe because they're longing for the opposite of The Evil. Maybe they've experienced The Evil in tangible ways, or have spent too much time warping their minds while tripping, so that they're more sensitive to the unseen world than other people; they've seen the colorful moving worlds of psychedelics and the fake love of opiates. Perhaps that's why they like angels so much. Or maybe angels are just doing what angels do and showing up when people need them the most.

When Stephan started inviting his friends over to hang out in our living room, study the Bible and pray like the Persian rug beneath them was sacrosanct, at first we worried that maybe they paid too much attention to ghosty, angely, demony kinds of things. One time Rick went along with them to hear someone they knew talk about God. Rick sat with some of The Lost Boys on the floor of an apartment across town and listened as things began to take a slow turn toward Crazy. Praying to angels and healing legs that didn't need healing to begin with and visions that didn't vibe with Scripture. I asked Rick how it was when he got home and he told me it was pretty messed up.

Even so, I'm sure that angels were rejoicing over Stephan. He'd left The Evil behind, and however young he was at the time, we truly believed he'd be okay; everything about him seemed new, and even though I know nothing guarantees a life of sobriety, it felt like we could literally see him walking forward. As though if I could stand him against a door frame, I'd be able to mark off every inch he grew. He began to read vociferously, and even though he was pretty cranky when he was quitting cigarettes for the fourth time, he loved people and he loved God. He and Rick talked at length about the tenants of the Christian faith. I kept making brownies for The Lost Boys and Stephan would hang out in the kitchen with me and talk.

* * *

One afternoon Rick was in the living room working on his computer and Stephan came in and dropped a handful of small deflated balloons in his lap, told him someone had given him heroin, that he didn't have the strength to part with it, and would you just get rid of it for me? Stephan left quickly and Rick sat staring at a handful of balloons that didn't look at all the way he'd imagined heroin looked like and thought about the odd chain of events that had led to a guy in full time ministry sitting in his living room with a pile of heroin in his lap. He went to the bathroom off of our kitchen, flushed them, and watched as they slowly swirled in the bowl before getting sucked down with a swallow to join all the other ugliness floating in the town's municipal sewer system. Drugs should never be flushed down the toilet because they can get in the water supply, but he didn't know that yet. The balloons were pink.

I'm not sure when it was that Stephan brought Waylen over for the first time, only that I came downstairs and found him sitting at the kitchen table with Stephan and a few other guys. Other than his long, curly hair, the thing to remember about Waylen is that he was big. He was about six feet, five inches tall, with broad shoulders, and even though his teeth were somewhat crooked, he had a beautiful smile. I liked him immediately. There was a certain anxiety about him, but he was gentle and without drugs he would have been perfectly at home in a Jane Austen novel. When Stephan introduced us he looked me in the eyes, smiled, and said "Hi, Mrs. James." In fact all of The Lost Boys, every one, were kind and polite and never avoided us. Quite the opposite, they seemed always ready to sit down and talk, cook with me in the kitchen, play whiffle ball with Rick, games in the living room. There were the stragglers, like the boy with the orange hair, but they hardly ever showed up.

That night, after Waylen left, Stephan came up to our bedroom, sat on our bed, and told us Waylen had been clean almost a month and needed a place to stay.

Almost in tandem, Rick and I agreed he could stay with us.

"Sure," I said, "of course he can stay here—he can stay in one of the beds in the basement."

Rick said, "Yeah, tell him he can stay here. I love Waylen," both of us assuming things would go down the same way they had for Stephan; a couple weeks detoxing in a chair then free and clear, a new life; it was easy to imagine Waylen free of drugs forever. And we had the space. Stephan said we should pray for Waylen so we did, but I wasn't really praying. I was thinking that the twin bed in the basement was so small his legs would hang off and I needed to put on clean sheets so he'd feel welcomed and how on earth would we feed him?

A few weeks later Rick asked if Stephan and Waylen wanted to go with him to Baltimore where he had a speaking engagement, so they rented a car, drove down, and stayed in a hotel for the night. When I asked Rick how it went, he told me he thought they'd both had a good time.

Later, Stephan told Rick Waylen used to be a big drug dealer.

"Seriously?"

"Yeah," Stephan said, "He was a pretty big deal."

"Like he carried a gun?"

"Of course."

"He doesn't still carry it, does he?"

"Probably," Stephan said. "I'm sure he had it when we went to Baltimore."

* * *

Rick and I had to go on an overnight trip. Waylen had been here for a few weeks at that point, and we'd just gotten a puppy we'd named Joey. I told Sweetboy it was okay if they had some friends over as long as there wasn't alcohol. I don't know why we trusted them so much, maybe because they were growing and seemed to be making good decisions and we wanted them to *know* we trusted them. As I'm writing this book it's been easy to shoot off a text to Stephan or Sweetboy or Jeremiah to confirm what I remember to be true. I just texted Stephan to see if there was alcohol that night, and he just got back to me and said there wasn't any.

We were in our hotel when we got the call, sometime in the early morning. It was Sweetboy.

"Hey, we can't find Joey."

Sweetboy, like me, would practically lay down his life for a dog, and the thought of a lost, defenseless puppy startled me completely awake.

"What? How long has he been gone?"

"We've looked everywhere."

"How long has he been gone?" I repeated.

"I don't know, an hour. I don't know."

"Where's the last place you saw him?"

"I thought he was inside. He must've gotten out somehow."

"And you looked everywhere . . . ?"

"Yes, we're in the backyard now and I think I just pissed off the neighbor. I was shining a flashlight around his backyard. So I just said 'my bad' and turned it off."

"Should I come home?" (I have no idea how that would have solved anything.)

"Nah, not yet."

"Okay, call me if you don't find him in half an hour. Okay?"

"Okay."

Twenty minutes later my phone rang. "Hey, we found him."

"Where was he?"

"He climbed into a laundry basket in the basement."

"Geeze. Okay, thanks for calling."

"Sure. Thanks, mom. See ya."

"Bye."

When we got home there was a message on our answering machine. It was the neighbor. He was angry and said the guys were out there all night making noise and they couldn't sleep. He said he hadn't seen any alcohol but they were being loud. I called back and apologized profusely. *I'm so sorry. We were out of town or we never would have let them be so loud if we were here.* They were cool about it once I called back, said they'd assumed we must have been gone. When I asked Sweetboy what they were doing out there, he said that they'd made bows and arrows and were shooting them all over the yard and it made me happy to think about them doing that, out on the lawn like cupids looking for the love of celestial beings.

Stephan told us that Waylen had said it was cool to see that you didn't need drugs to have fun. It was a few weeks later that he moved out and I didn't see him again for a very long time. He left a pair of shorts in the basement but that was it.

It took me a while before the irony of the bows and arrows occurred to me; The Lost Boys shooting arrows like addicts shooting heroin.

This was all before our home began to rumble like the beginnings of a rocket launch destined to U-turn into the earth, of ambulances and critical care units, but still, they had a fun time that night.

PATTERNS

CHESS IS A UTILITARIAN GAME; stripped first of pawns then knight then castle, a player wins by slowing down, measuring each step and figuring out what works best. But there's charm too—the elegance of dark plus light side by side and the hint of shine from the ivory, the decussated board, the gentle touch of fingers before the hushed sound of felt sliding across it. Patterns evolve and expand as the pieces are moved, and if each of them glowed red and a camera, shutter open, hung above them and captured the movement in one long blink, the result would be a crisscross of lines, rectangles, and squares, stars on stars on stars.

It was a year before I found the text on Sweetboy's phone from the drug dealer. Rick was in his office and it was around 11:00 p.m. A few months earlier Sweetboy had had a conversation with Rick and told him he'd been using drugs. He didn't say what drugs, but we were encouraged that he'd told us. He said he would stop. We assumed that he'd started smoking marijuana, maybe something else, something innocuous. We didn't know what he was doing, only that he'd told us he would stop.

It wasn't too cold or too hot. The Lost Boys were up in The Chill Spot. Waylen had moved out months earlier. At that point Christopher and Stephan were living with us and the Bible study had continued to grow. Rick was working on a complicated piece of writing that compared Paul's statement in 2 Corinthians 2:11—"So that we would not be outwitted by Satan; for we are not ignorant of his designs"—with the game of chess. He was writing about pattern recognition and making the point that much like chess, over time and with practice, the patterns of The Evil can be recognized and its next move anticipated. He was deep in thought, and since Rick has attention surplus disorder like I have attention deficit disorder, he was oblivious to the world. But then suddenly, like some supernatural nudge, he thought he should check on The Lost Boys.

There's a railing around the top of the stairs in The Chill Spot that obstructs your view until you're standing in the room. The Lost Boys had pushed an oversized couch into the middle of the space, facing the round window and the picture of Jesus that I'd drawn a smile on, and dragged the rug and coffee table in front of it. Jeremiah, Christopher, Max, and Sam were there. When Rick reached the top of the stairs, he saw Sweetboy quickly brush something off a chessboard and tuck it next to the couch. But just like the moment before, in his office when he felt like he should check on them, Rick felt a sudden ache of affection for his son. He went to him, leaned over, kissed him on the head, said, "I love you," and left. That's all he did. The heterodoxy of this still baffles me.

Every drug counselor and Al-Anon member everywhere would say this was a stupid thing to do, that Rick should have grabbed the board, looked for more drugs, taken Sweetboy inside, and signed him up for rehab. I would have too. But now, years later, I'm not sure it would have been. It wasn't a decision, it was something that happened. It was—be it an unusual one—a response; as though the Holy Spirit had come over Rick and his options suddenly narrowed down to this one small act of physical affection. I think the visceral love of his father had a greater effect on Sweetboy than a lecture and rehab would have. In some strange way, I think what Rick did (or didn't do) opened communication more than closed it. Sweetboy understood that he could be honest with his father and nothing would ever change his love for him.

Jeremiah told us he'd never seen the love of Christ like he did that night.

* * *

Parents will go to great subconscious efforts to believe their child is not doing drugs; we can miss the most obvious things: *Mom, my phone was stolen, can you buy me a new one?* for a mother, means his phone was stolen and he needs a new one, and *I lost all my textbooks* means he lost his textbooks and needs money to buy more. It often doesn't occur to parents, at least in the beginning stages, that their child is lying to get money for drugs. In fact, many years ago when I was just a teenager, one of my friend's brothers had gotten into drugs and was in a rehab program. At Christmas her mother told us how awful it was, because all the gifts her brother had bought were stolen out of his car. Of course they gave him money to buy new ones.

If you're a parent and your child has turned out squeaky clean, got into the great college, with the great scholarship, and the great friends, never a blunt having touched his lips, please refrain from judgment, because if that same child's grades were falling and there were small bits of tinfoil lying around his room, good chance you'd think the teachers didn't understand how brilliant he was and the foil was left over from his lunch bag. At least at first you'd think that.

Two months after Rick found Sweetboy in The Chill Spot, after he'd snorted a crushed pill off a chessboard, and after we'd had numerous conversations with him about staying away from drugs, Sweetboy asked if he could talk to us.

We were in the kitchen and some of The Lost Boys were sitting on the porch in the Adirondack chairs smoking. It was a hot day and the air conditioner in our dining room was on full blast but the cold air wasn't making it around the corner into the kitchen. I kept going around the corner and standing in front of the window unit, holding my hair off my shoulders to cool off. Christopher was outside, and Sam, Jeremiah, Stephan, and Sweetboy. After a while I heard them head into the garage. Rick and I had been praying out loud, something we'd begun to do impromptu after Jules left. Sweetboy came into the kitchen.

"Hey, can I talk to you guys for a minute?"

I felt my heart warm to my son because it was him, the Sweetboy I knew, and when he said that to us for some reason, I found myself tearing up. His kindness, his thoughtfulness. He'd drifted from us, but I loved him so much.

"Sure," Rick said, and grabbed a Fresca from the pantry before he went outside. I followed him, feeling a little nervous, a little lightheaded, a feeling that would eventually become very familiar to me. We sat down.

Sweetboy sat down opposite us, lit a cigarette, and put his head in his hands.

He was silent.

"What's up?" Rick said.

"I need to tell you something."

I'm not sure why, because it made sense that it would be related to drugs, but I asked him if he was gay.

"No," and he didn't laugh or even smile and I knew right then that whatever he told us would shock us more than if he'd told us he was gay. We were concerned about drugs but we were still shuffling around in a parental fog, the pill and the chessboard was a onetime thing. He and Rick talked about how he was doing, we thought he'd been honest about everything.

"What are you doing?" Rick said.

"Heroin."

It was a simple word, and the scariest one I'd ever heard. It sat outside of my brain for a moment before wiggling into my cortex and lying prone, as though waiting for what was next. *Heroin.*

My body grew cold and I covered my mouth like some kind of stupid mother who sees a mouse in the kitchen. Tears immediately sprung to my eyes. "No," I said. "Sweetboy, no." I half yelled.

He wiped away a tear.

"You have to go to rehab," I said. I had no idea yet that rehab doesn't always work, that sometimes they are only revolving doors that suck people in until they spit them out until they suck them in again.

"I can't."

It wasn't *I won't*, it wasn't *no*, it was *I can't*. He was telling the truth. He wanted to stop but he couldn't go to rehab; he knew he wouldn't be able to stay. "You can go to IOP," I said. IOP stands for Intensive Outpatient rehab.

Rick repeated that he needed to go to IOP and began to explain that we would test him. He said we would help him and that everything would be okay, *we'll help you, it will be okay*, while Sweetboy sat across from us with his head down.

I pushed rehab. At that point I assumed rehab was the only hope someone who used heroin had. I wasn't aware of any other options to treat opiate addiction. Anything I knew about heroin was because of what Stephan told us, and he'd told us a lot: about his friends who had died and were in prison, about how it ruined so many lives, and how hard it was to quit. I think in retrospect, some of what compelled me to immediately push rehab was that I felt completely unable to handle things. I knew nothing about heroin and if he was at home I might miss something. I didn't want to be a part of anything right then. I wanted to disappear and then come back and everything would be normal again. Someone else, some expert, would handle things and he would come home sober and healed forever.

But Rick thought he should stay here and we should test him. He was right and I knew it. I knew there was no way Sweetboy would stay at rehab, that he would run as soon as we dropped him off. And there was more support here. He could talk to us, and Stephan and Christopher. They would encourage him and pray with him. I went inside, still crying, opened my computer, and began searching for a site that sold drug tests in bulk.

* * *

Considering what I know now, I'm glad we didn't send him to rehab and that we chose instead to test him here every day. Even though in some ways—in light of his overdose—the outcome was tragic, I believe it would have been worse if we'd insisted on rehab at that point because I'm not sure we would have ever seen him again. I think he would have run. My initial inclination was to send him far away, somewhere in Montana or North Dakota, where he'd have to hike ten miles a day and eat food from a mess hall, sit in circles and bemoan each other's troubles, but I'm glad we didn't send him away. I don't think Sweetboy would have been a good candidate. For him, it was important to be home to get better. We were close. He trusted us. He trusted his friends; *we* trusted his friends. (The Lost Boys were the ones who said he should tell us he was doing heroin.) If we didn't know his friends so well, or they used too, perhaps it would have been best to send him away.

Please don't misunderstand me. Rehab can be a good option, but I do think it's important to pause and try to understand where a person's heart is, to make sure they know you love them no matter what. And pray. Of course you have to pray, because if you're not praying you might miss an opportunity to kiss your child on the head.

* ✳ *

One time I was flying back from a conference and I looked out the window and saw nickel colored rivers curving all over the green earth like silver cords dropped from miles up. I rested my head on the cool window and looked. It was so peaceful. And I felt as though God was saying to me, "Look what I've done." For a long time I just stared down in awe. And then the plane began its descent and I began to see the usual warehouse roofs and then other machinations of the present age, roads and cars, and we came in lower still, the engines of the plane gunning as though in some kind of earnest backpedaling slant, and the wheels going down and the flaps raising and lowering as the wings evened out. And then we flew low over a river and a port, and ships I felt I could touch, large and magnificent, hulls the size of mountains, water pouring from their holes as bilge was pumped out. I am only one of them, I thought.

WITHOUT CEASING

EVERY NIGHT RICK and I lay on our bed, held hands, and prayed: for Sweetboy and Jules and Sophie, for Christopher, Stephan, Jeremiah, for Waylen and The Lost Boys in general. Sometimes Stephan would come up and lie on our bed with us and we'd pray for someone he told us about. There were times when he'd disappear for a few days and I'd begin to worry, but he always came back, often with someone he wanted us to meet. One time he brought over a large guy with dark hair and after that he would drop by from time to time. He was close to seven feet tall and muscular, as though embedded at birth with some kind of industrial strength bionic gene. He had a beard that went from ear to ear, missing his upper lip the way Amish men wear them. He dressed neatly in polo shirts and striped blue button downs that seemed almost antithetical to his size and build, but his face was soft and he was prone to tear up. When I first met him I told him he reminded me of the Jolly Green Giant and we both laughed. I could tell he was used to comments like that.

I'll always remember him because—as though his physical strength required a gentle soul—he listened and asked questions and seemed to care about others more than himself. One fall evening I was in the kitchen doing dishes when he walked by the window with a big smile. He was wearing a bright yellow shirt and when he came in, he leaned back against the counter to chat. For some reason the overhead light in the kitchen wasn't on, so the room was darker than usual. At that point the original kitchen window was above the sink, one of those louvered ones they used to use in the 1950s, with horizontal panes of glass that open and close with a crank. In the winter it let in a lot of cold air.

"How are you?" he said when he came in the door. His questions were never in passing, but earnest, and when I was with him I always felt like he was the only person in the world I could open up to.

I had left the dishes and was leaning against the stove. "Good. Good. How are you?"

He told me he was going through a hard time and began explaining a project he'd been working on that wasn't working out.

His back was facing the window, so that each pane of glass reflected a yellow strip of his shirt making it look somehow digitized. As he was telling me how difficult it was to be failing at a project he'd been working so hard on, and how he thought it would affect his younger brother who had been helping him, I felt an urge to pray for him and I did, silently, as we stood there talking. Then my prayer turned into a desire to talk to him about God, and Jesus. To talk to him about my faith.

So I did. And he listened, his soft face attentive and beginning to tear up. Suddenly I was the girl in the city standing on a corner with a placard that reads *Jesus Saves*. I wasn't myself and yet I was completely myself. I felt a great love for him, but even so, I wondered if what I was saying sounded weird, like I was one of those people who climb up mountains with a handful of like-mindeds and wait for God to come back and scoop them up in a spinning disk with tiny windows and a white flash like an atom bomb with a ring of halo-smoke spreading out above it. But the fact was, if I didn't tell him about Christ, then I didn't believe it myself; that, or I couldn't care less about him. And I did care about him. I loved him, and I'd prayed for him, so I had to tell him these things. Logic dictated it, and so did my love.

The next evening, he drank too much whiskey and sped down a dark narrow street with a friend and flipped his car and died. When Stephan told me, I didn't believe it because he seemed too big to die. He was as large as an angel. His face was a confidant's. He wore polo shirts and liked people. He wasn't the type of person who dies.

* * *

After Sweetboy told us he was doing heroin, I started a prayer group at church. One time I prayed and cried so hard that snot poured out of my nose. We prayed sitting around a large table in the library, and there were floor-to-ceiling bookcases sectioned off according to topic: theology, concordances, spiritual life, parenting. There was an anachronistic Dewey Decimal Card System catalog on a desk that had cards with penciled dates going back as far as the 1970s.

So we prayed for our children as snot ran from my nose, and we didn't judge because we would have had to have had some psychotic break, some Holden Caulfield *phoniness, if you want to know the truth,* to think our addicted kid was better than anyone else's addicted kid. I prayed mostly for Sweetboy to love God, that whatever faith was in him would catch fire and grow.

* * *

St. Paul says to pray *without ceasing* so I started doing it. Prayer was something I'd waxed on about for years but didn't completely get. Although I had always prayed, I wasn't one of those people who prostrate themselves in expectation of God's next work. Prayer was a part of my life, but it was easygoing and comfortable.

If you back up enough to see the full picture of time—of eternity—and acknowledge all that we *don't* see from our perspective, it certainly flattens the playing field. Here I sit in my comfortable house with my laptop and coffee wondering what we'll have for dinner, while a woman on the other side of town is calling out to God for help while she detoxes on her couch because she wants to be a better mother. She's calling for him and calling for him because she knows he's her only hope; even though he's the one who takes, he's also the one who gives. The one who loves and the one who saves.

I often think that eternally speaking, a woman pleading with God to get her off heroin is better off than a woman planning her next meal. Seeking God is always better than not seeking God no matter what the circumstances, and while I'd already been praying for years when I first learned Sweetboy had tried heroin, I'd never been to that place where—like the woman I imagine on the couch trying to quit—I felt every pang and gag and twitch of pain and had to beg God to save me, until I understood how possible it was that we could lose him. I suppose what I'm getting at here is that, as it says in Psalm 34, "The LORD is near to the brokenhearted," and that being brokenhearted is a fruitful place to be.

God used Sweetboy's addiction to teach me to seek him in a way I'd never had to. And as I called out to God, I began to see him everywhere. God's effect is in the sky, the seasons, rocks, turtles, Waylen, Stephan, Sweetboy, love. These are the things God used to show me he was way close to my broken heart.

* * *

I often did yard work as I prayed. We have a large yard. I enjoy being outside and I find the methodical act of gathering sticks or raking leaves to be consolatory, as though retrieving nature's detritus gives me the dulled humor of an obedient animal at work, the way a beaver might go about making a dam, one stick at a time, head half above the water.

One afternoon I was gathering sticks and leaves from an area of our yard that's far from our house, and piling them onto an old bed of ash where our neighbor had been burning yard waste earlier in the week. Tim and his wife, Carol, are friends and we burn our brush together every fall. Sometimes the fire reaches over my head as we throw things in.

That afternoon there was a slight breeze, and whenever I threw sticks on the pile they kicked up a small cloud of old ash. After working for an hour or so I tossed on the last of the branches and went inside. I would light the pile later in the week.

Certain things in the Bible seem to take on the significance of a protagonist in light of whatever spectacular thing they personify— gold, smoke, blood, fire—and while I wasn't praying for gold thrones or chariots, I had become more sensitive to the things around me. Since

I was praying so much, I was listening too—looking for how God might be speaking to me.

Two days after I'd gathered the sticks and put them on the pile in the backyard, I was pacing the rooms upstairs. We hadn't heard from Sweetboy for a while. I kept walking from my studio to his room, and looking out his window where I could see the driveway, praying the oh-so-familiar prayers: that he hadn't done heroin, that he was okay, that he would return. We'd been faithfully testing him, but by that time I'd started researching things related to heroin and learned about The Badlands and the tents next to the train tracks and the sometimes dead bodies from overdoses; The Evil and all that it entailed felt like an enormous shirred coat sinking ever lower to muffle what it could. I imagined a gang of one, some half-grown kid digging in his pocket for a ziplock and handing it to Sweetboy—no words, just Sweetboy with his folded bills, and then the dope, and then some corner or basement stairs split in half by shadows from the streetlights where he would go shoot up.

I went to a window that overlooks our backyard. Looking out that window always comforts me. I've wondered if it's because everything out there is created. I wonder if other people feel relief when they look at backyards, if backyards comfort them too. Maybe I feel comforted because it's a reminder of the expanse beyond me, like the way God answered Job's cries and questions by pointing out the seas and leviathans he'd made, his creation so obvious that we miss it. As though God wants us to remember he's standing right in front of us in all his majesty even as we huddle scared behind our window shades. He's a big God and he's in control. When I go outside, even in the bitter cold, I always feel better.

As I looked out, what looked like smoke was rising from the stick pile I'd made earlier in the week; perhaps the wind had kicked up a little ash. I was distracted by worry. I went back to praying. I looked at my phone in case Sweetboy had texted; I lay down on my bed and prayed some more. I got up and went downstairs to see if Rick had gotten a message (he hadn't). I went back upstairs and saw a message on my phone. It was from our neighbor, Carol:

"Hi, it's Carol. Are you burning sticks in the back? Because the pile's on fire and I didn't see anyone back there." She laughed, "It's a little strange."

I looked out. By that time the flames were high, reaching up that way flames do—hurried and anxious, like they're trying to grab something they can't quite reach. I stared at the oddness of it. It shocked me. It had come out of nowhere as though God himself had lit it. It was filled with God's power the way leviathans are filled with God's power, and I knew immediately that it was a manifestation of a spiritual reality. God was listening and somehow Sweetboy's faith would grow the way those flames grew out of nothing. It was one of those moments of unexpected peace, like the way the healthy waves of an ECG can calm your heart even as you watch them jolt up and down.

I thanked God and opened my Bible. I'd been reading through the New Testament so I opened to where I'd left off, and started reading. Tucked into the first chapter of 2 Timothy, I read, *For this reason I remind you to fan into flame the gift of God.*

A few weeks later I woke up to almost audible words: *It's not a scheme, it's a loving plan.* Peace like a river.

PEE TEST

DRUG TESTS AREN'T LIKE PREGNANCY TESTS. There are the same indicative lines (blue or red usually, not pink) but rather than a plastic stick, they are attached to the sides of T-cups, a plastic cup a little larger than a jigger glass. They're also a lot more complicated than a pregnancy test. The drugs are abbreviated (AMP, BAR, BUP, EDDP, etc.) and false positives aren't unprecedented. Certain antidepressants can cause a false negative. A bit of research is necessary if you want to avoid a false negative; I don't think it would take long to find any information needed on the internet, false negatives of course being the most important thing to prevent, as they make the whole process pointless. You can buy tests that test for only a few drugs, or you can buy tests that test for a whole string of them. The more drugs they test for, the more expensive the test, so unless you just received federal money for some kind of research grant, cost can be prohibitive. There are the more inexpensive tests that only test for a few drugs (opiates, cocaine, marijuana), and there are tests with more extensive panels that include obscure and less abused drugs like propoxyphene and synthetic marijuana. The lines appear horizontally, lined up according to drug on one side of the cup. Sometimes when reading a test a line will be faded slightly, but since it's a visible line, even though it might be faint, it's still negative. That's what the directions tell you. It's tempting to think if the line is very, very faint that it's positive, but the directions say if there's any line at all it's negative. But why is it faded? Is it because there's a barely detectible amount of an abusable drug floating around in the pee?

I settled on a ten-panel drug test of average size—not for the beginner but not for the advanced drug abuser either: *cocaine, marijuana, PCP, amphetamines, opiates, benzodiazepines, barbiturates, methadone, propoxyphene, and Quaaludes.* The tests arrived on our doorstep in large unmarked cardboard boxes. The boxes were light, and if I shook them, they clattered like a bunch of Sunday school kids running around in a church gym. The directions were printed on a large sheet of thin paper folded into sixteen squares. When I got the tests, I spread the sheet out on the floor, flattened it with my knees, and ran a finger under each line of directions so I wouldn't miss anything.

* ✳ *

Ways to pass a pee test: strap pipette of someone else's clean pee to leg under jeans; drink copious amounts of water two to three hours before test (but careful, too much can be fatal); take Midol; take a handful of aspirin four hours before test (don't worry it will only make you light headed); chug cranberry juice; spike pee with bleach.

LOST

WE WERE TESTING SWEETBOY and he passed every time. It appeared he would be okay. I wondered often about what could have happened if he'd never told us he'd been using. He'd been hanging out with Stephan and Christopher and Jeremiah, which encouraged us because they didn't use and cared about Sweetboy—it was Stephan and Jeremiah who had made him sit down and tell us what he was doing.

In light of the clean tests and the fact that Stephan would be here too, Rick and I thought it would be okay to go to Orlando for a work-related conference. It was our first trip after learning he'd been doing heroin and even though outwardly things seemed fine, I was anxious—I felt like I was stepping into a space between control and ever-after, hoping that The Evil's sudden, overexposed image had already faded to nothing.

The exit doors of baggage claim at Orlando International Airport are like a bank of crystal eyelids; wide-as-cars panes of glass humming open and closed interspersed with the faster, winking turns of revolving glass doors to keep the cold air in. When we left the cool of the airport there was a small fountain and the soft gurgle of it combined with what seemed like a warmth that had been waiting for us. Even though I've always hated Orlando with its plastic renditions of things so beautiful they should never be rendered in plastic, it somehow felt peaceful to me.

When we got to the hotel, Rick went to the room to lie down and I took the rental car to meet some friends at an Outback Steakhouse.

By then it was dark. I could see the lights from the main tourist strip, International Drive, lighting the sky, and two skylights hidden somewhere in the area were sweeping across the sky, almost from horizon to horizon. My GPS directed me to get on I-4. I thought you took 408 to the Outback, but maybe we were meeting at a different one.

After an uncomfortably long time on what I thought was I-4, any warmth or fountain-bubbly goodness I'd felt at the airport was gone. I found myself on some lonely interstate that seemed so inconsequential the satellites wouldn't pick it up. The wafting smell of orange blossoms had faded and the sturdy, thousands-of-dollars nursery-grown palm trees that framed the many stucco buildings were gone. Once I got the hint from the orangeless, treeless, quickly oxidizing landscape, and realized I was lost, I took an exit to turn around, but instead found myself on a flat dirt road with only a few small houses propped on cement blocks that were without description, without plants or porches or obvious driveways—they looked like long ago failed local insurance agencies, converted garages. I stopped in front of what was less a house than a shack.

I called Rick.

"I'm lost."

"What about GPS?"

"It's not working. I think there might be alligators nearby."

"Where were you supposed to meet them?"

"One of those Outback places."

"In Orlando? You mean in the city?"

"I hate Outback Steakhouse," I said. "It's so loud. I don't even want to go."

"Just turn around."

"I *did*," I said, "but I can't find the highway."

"Okay, I'll look it up . . . What's the name of the street?"

"I don't *know!*"

"Wait, hold on, I'm getting another call."

I looked at the house and did a slow U-turn in the dirt.

He came back on, "Okay. Turn around and head back."

"I already did." I started to cry a little.

"Hold on, I got another call."

"Why do you keep taking it?" I said, even as he put me on hold. I slowly drove to the next street where I could see a street sign and took a left. By the time he got back on I'd found the highway and was headed back. "Never mind, I'm good. I'll see you soon."

When I got back to the room, Rick was lying on the bed with his hands behind his head staring at the ceiling. He didn't look at me. I lay down next to him and propped myself up on a pillow. "What's wrong?"

He continued staring at the ceiling. "Sweetboy called while we were on the phone. I didn't want you to worry so I didn't say anything, but I wanted you to come back." My heart sank, and my elbow felt loose, like it might give way.

"He was in Philly with Christopher and a cop pulled him over. When he called he handed the cop the phone and when he got on he said they were in a part of Philly they shouldn't be in. He said it's basically an open-air drug market."

I was silent.

"The only reason they had to be there was to buy drugs. The cop said they looked like they hadn't been using long and he thought if he stopped them maybe they wouldn't come back to the area and wouldn't get addicted." He finally looked at me. "He searched their car but didn't find anything so he couldn't arrest him. He told Sweetboy to call us." Rick spoke quietly and slowly, like there were a thousand sighs under his breath.

"Call him back," I said, "Call Sweetboy back." Rick quietly picked up the phone and dialed. When he picked up, Rick said I wanted to talk to him.

I took the phone and said the only thing I could think of, "*Why? Sweetboy, why?*" There was some slipstream he had dipped into, and it seemed like the beginning of the end to me; once someone starts going into the city to get heroin they've become desperate for the stuff. Of course, it's plenty easy to get heroin in the suburbs or farmlands, but cities fit my *Run Nicky Run* narrative, and the truth is, it's faster to score dope in cities, and although dangerous, it's easier too. I could practically see the litter strewn corners and makeshift tents. I repeated, "*Why?*"

"I don't know."

"Where are you now?"

"Headed back home."

We caught the next flight back. Rick sat down with Sweetboy and he told Rick he'd prayed as they drove to Philly that God would stop them because he didn't want to buy heroin but felt like he had to, like he needed it, and it was starting to scare him. He was still shaken up a little when they talked. Months later he would tell us that one time when he went into Kensington and pulled out fifty dollars to give a dealer, a junkie ran up and yanked the money from his hand. Just like that. I don't know if he prayed that time—either way he didn't get his heroin.

* * *

This morning when I woke up I couldn't remember the way our solar system works. Sometimes my memory will cut out on the most basic things, things I've known forever, and other times I'll remember the way the cuff of someone's pant leg was half turned up weeks earlier, but this morning as I lay in bed whatever drawings or papier-mâché models I made in grade school had failed me because I was suddenly unable to remember whether we circled the moon or the moon circled us. I had dreamt I was looking out the living room window—top row, fourth pane from the left—at the moon, which was split neatly in half, that specific moment in its cycle when you're able, if you look closely, to make out the shadowed half as well as the lit half. I was just standing at the window looking at the moon. When I woke up I couldn't remember how the solar system works, what sphere orbits what sphere, so I went upstairs and asked Rick. Of course, the smaller orb always circles the larger one: moon circles us, we circle sun, and I felt stupid for asking, but Rick answered me without hesitation or judgment. I think there's comfort in translating things as vast and complicated as the universe into things as controllable as marbles and papier-mâché planets. I prayed for my children—those three stars of Orion's belt—as complex as they are, because I believe the one who made them knows them, and the one who knows them loves them, and whether it's Saturn's halo or Cassiopeia his plans are fantastical and are sprouted from the seed of love.

* * *

The testing continued. Now Rick stood outside the bathroom door and waited for the T-cups. It was my job to read them. I usually took them upstairs and held them up to the light to make sure I read the lines correctly. It's almost comical for me to use the term "older and wiser," but I'd be justified if I decided to use it on every page of this book: *In retrospect. If only I knew what I know now when I was younger. Hindsight.* Before I read each test I would feel the cup to make sure it was warm, that it was authentic urine and he hadn't snuck in someone else's pee. It was always warm so I assumed it was his. Sweetboy recently told me he just ran hot water over the cup to warm it before he gave it to me. I can easily picture one of those big fat blow up hammers clobbering my head like in a cartoon. The caption would say, *Duh, I dunno, what?*

Two days after we got back from Florida I was standing on the back porch watering flowers when Sweetboy and Christopher pulled into the driveway.

"Hey," Sweetboy said, and went inside. Christopher was about to follow him but I went around to his side of the car.

"Christopher, you can't do that, you can't do stuff like that."

He knew I meant their trip to the city. He looked at me, "I can stop hanging out with him if you want."

But I didn't want that. "No," I said, "you're his best friend. No." For some reason the thought of Sweetboy without Christopher grieved me. "But you can't do stuff like that anymore. You have to take care of him. Please take care of him, don't let him do stuff like that." I trusted Christopher, and while in retrospect I wouldn't have been naive with the pee tests, I would still tell Christopher to take care of him. The conversation was short and sad. We were in front of the garage door.

At some point Christopher came upstairs and stood next to Rick's side of the bed. Rick was on his computer and I was reading. Rick asked how he was and after a short silence, he said, "I'm sorry." Rick reached his arms up and Christopher bent down and they hugged.

It was a long hug. When he stood back up, I think I saw him wipe a tear from his face, then he went back downstairs.

Christopher started reading the Bible. He stopped following Sweetboy every time he went outside for a smoke when Rick was in the living room talking to a handful of Lost Boys. He began paying attention. He'd been more into psychedelics than opiates, but his mind was still sharp. He became interested in things—religion, philosophy, theology. At one point he told Rick that it was because of the things he and Sweetboy had talked about before they'd started doing heavy drugs that he knew what it was to be a Christian and that he was a Christian because of Sweetboy.

* ✳ *

I learned recently from a birder friend that pigeons are a kind of dove because they belong to the Columbidae bird family. Some people call city pigeons flying rats because there are so many of them and they congregate wherever food congregates: next to garbage cans, behind restaurants, in city parks. We have a mourning dove in the trees next to our driveway. You can hear it in the morning—a low note flipping to a higher note and then back down to three lower notes that sound as though they're coming from a wooden whistle. I saw the dove on a long branch once, and while it's light brown, whereas pigeons are gray, the shape is the same. They have small heads and long necks. I find it fascinating that the same type of bird that peppers dirty city streets is the same type of bird that showed up on Jesus' shoulder as the Holy Spirit. Something about the Holy Spirit makes you rejoice and also mourn. The Holy Spirit gives us wisdom and fills us with peace, but sometimes it means we grieve. There's a mysterious sadness and a joy in this.

After Waylen lived with us for that short time—when he made bows and arrows with The Lost Boys and shot them into the night in our backyard and laughed and yelled, when Rick took him and Stephan to hear the talk he was giving at the university—we thought he was still doing okay. At first, Stephan spent time with him and tried to encourage him to stay clean, but after a while he stopped hanging out with him—maybe because there wasn't a whole lot he could do.

After he left there were two times he came back, although at one point I did see him at a friend's Bible study. The first time he showed back up he was high and Rick went out to the driveway and told him he couldn't come in and that he needed to leave. It kills me that Rick had to tell him to leave, as though Waylen only wanted to come home but we wouldn't let him. Even now, when I think about him not being allowed in our house it can make me cry. The other time he showed up he was sober, but barely, it had only been a few weeks. That's when Rick sat down with him, both of them in the Adirondack chairs on that sunny day, Waylen in his aviators and ponytail, and they prayed together and then later that same day Rick told me about the tear that ran down his cheek. Rick also told him if he didn't stop doing heroin he'd be dead in a year. I had said the same thing when I ran into him at the Bible study. It's the first thing that came to my mind. I looked at him and said, "You have to stop using, Waylen. You could die." I didn't want him to die.

One Tuesday night when we were at the prayer group at the church, Rick got off his chair, turned around, knelt, and begged God to save Waylen. A few months after he did that, Waylen was driving without a license and hit a woman. She almost died and was in the hospital for months. She wrote him a letter saying she forgave him. He went to prison after that.

THE RUIN OF TAPESTRIES
AND COUCHES

SOPHIE AND NEIL got married on June 2nd and the reception was in our backyard. Rick and I and some of The Lost Boys spent most of the next day folding up tables and chairs and taking down string lights. I went around and picked up random things like stray flowers or spoons that had fallen on the grass. It was a sunny day, and cool. I didn't know where Sweetboy was, but I wasn't worried since it had been months since he and Christopher had been stopped by the cop and he was still testing clean. There were large garbage cans in the garage where I was throwing the garbage, and on one of my trips in I decided to check out The Chill Spot. I think Rick had been going up, but it had been a while since I'd looked around. Both windows were open; the large one and the round one with Jesus under it. Even with the windows open it smelled of smoke. The ashtrays, which included a few glasses filled with water, were full of cigarette butts, and there was a cluster of Red Bulls like blue bowling pins on the floor next to the couch. The cigarette butts always made me sad. We should never have let Sweetboy smoke . . . I think it's that last thought that made me destroy The Chill Spot; that thought that we could have done something different to prevent Sweetboy from using heroin. It was another *if only* and that, combined with the stink and aura of the place, made me launch into a destructive fury.

I tugged off cushions, tore pictures off the walls, and entangled myself in string lights. I smashed a hookah, almost begging the thing to cut me—I ransacked the place and would have pulled down the dusty beams if I could. I ripped down a tapestry, pushed the TV onto the floor, and swung the game controllers by their cords, like rocks in a sling, across the room. I still look back on that purging of things fondly. Sometimes I even fantasize about it. Rick and I have always made a point as parents to allow for the vast areas of gray; morality is a morality of the heart as much as actions. Is Janis Joplin's music evil and David Crowder's righteous? It depends on what you do with it, where your heart wanders to. But as I ransacked every corner of The Chill Spot, I saw things as black and white because there was satisfaction in that, I was the one in control, and I parsed out every place, every item, like garbage into recycle bins: plastic, glass, paper. The mind games I played that afternoon in The Chill Spot were my relief, as though in dividing objects, I could replicate the past and stamp things approved or disapproved. Good or bad.

Now what's left of The Chill Spot is only wood and boards. There is no carpet or tapestries or chairs. No ashtrays or Mario Brothers or couch, but if I go up there it still reminds me of The Evil. Good vs. Bad, one vampy switch-hitting bit takes on the maker of the universe, or billions of universes—perhaps time will tell. Now, in The Chill Spot of my mind, one chair goes to one side, another chair goes to the other. Coffee table and paintings one way, ashtray and hookah another. Good or bad, every object had a declension and its proper space was assigned. Every entity in the room was a personification of The Evil. And as The Evil is quantified in myriad ways, each object's personality had a certain cast; gray-green-red-ochre, the bare wooden studs might as well have been breathing sour breath into the room, swelling with the faint fog of mildew that powdered the beams with a dust of white, because eventually my brain and my heart lined up and I went on that rampage because my anger gave me superhuman strength.

One month after I destroyed The Chill Spot Sophie would chase an ambulance through town as Rick and I prayed that God would keep Sweetboy alive.

NEXT OF KIN

As they were rushing Sweetboy into the emergency room we were trying to touch him. Rick had his hand on his arm. Since they had intubated him and tubes and tape were pressed down on his face like a plastic palm, his nose and mouth and even his eyes were virtually invisible. There was a bag, blue or clear, I can't remember, and I think one of the EMTs held it as they were pushing the stretcher, but perhaps that's only something I saw on a TV show once. Someone said, "We had to intubate him," I remember, which seemed to mean it was unusual to do it—that word, *had*, is what rose up from my numb brain.

I think it was the first clear word I heard, like everything had been silent outside but when we went through the doors of the emergency room I could hear again. Maybe because of the hospital environment, as though I was suddenly back in the emergency room when Sweetboy was three and sitting on my lap sipping cherry flavored charcoal through a straw to absorb the iron from the bottle of chewable vitamins plus iron he'd swallowed, listening carefully to the doctor so I wouldn't miss anything. I was used to paying attention in the hospital. I don't believe in omens. Instead, I'll use the word *intimation*. That sounds better. His need for the sweet taste of chewable vitamins was intimation of future events.

After I heard someone say "we had to intubate him," I could see that his face was less blue. He had a pulse. He was alive. I remember the blue or clear bag, I remember lines and cords and then doctors and nurses and audible beeps but I don't know if the beeps had anything to do with Sweetboy or if they were coming from somewhere behind a curtain, a man being monitored for a heart attack perhaps, or maybe the beeps I heard weren't real but only what I imagined emergency rooms sounded like, the scrubs and swinging doors and monitors and complicated medical things. Rick was keeping up with the gurney, and suddenly bent over in an attempt to hold him. He pressed his body to Sweetboy's, cupped his face in both hands and said, "Don't leave me, Sweetboy, please, don't leave me. You're my best friend." Those are the next clear words I heard. The paramedics stopped the gurney when he did this. They paused, like they knew it might be the last opportunity for a father to say goodbye to his son. Then, as soon as Rick stood up, they quickly pushed Sweetboy through the emergency room doors.

That image, of Rick leaning over on top of his son and telling him not to die because he was his best friend—if there's one memory I'd like to forget it's that one. After they pushed him through the doors, someone gently led us into a small, windowless room. There were comfortable chairs and three side tables with tissue boxes on them. It was a clean room but it felt like there was a skim of something in it, like every family that had ever received bad news and bent over crying, rocking into their own laps, had left their tears deposited into the corners where they turned to mist and dispersed for the next group to inhale. I felt a strange desperation and despondency that seemed oddly unrelated to Sweetboy. In *The Year of Magical Thinking*, Didion says that the initial responses to death are shock, numbness, and disbelief. In that windowless room my first thoughts—fleeting as they were— weren't centered on what I was beginning to realize could be the death of my son, but on the other spouses or parents or whoever, that had sat in those same chairs and experienced shock, numbness, and disbelief. It was odd how I wasn't thinking about our situation yet. I was somewhere between shock and numbness. The room was mauve and had fluorescent lighting. I hate the color mauve.

Some of The Lost Boys were already there. They looked fragile and I wanted to hug every one of them but I thought if I did they might disappear and I needed them. If they were alive Sweetboy was alive; it seemed impossible that Sweetboy could die if they were still here. It was the first of many superstitions. They all looked stunned and also sorrowful. Jeremiah, Christopher, Sam, and others I don't remember were there. I could hear a commotion on the other side of the emergency room doors whenever they opened. I think I heard someone yell, but then when I tried to listen I heard nothing.

Eventually a woman wearing a white coat came in. "They're working on him," she said. This is exactly what we were told by the paramedics when they were in the pool house and this time, instead of falling to my knees, I asked if he was going to be okay. *We're working on him.* I was beginning to understand that was how they prepared someone for the worst. It was the standard protocol. There're also the even more grief-begetting words *next of kin.* After a plane crash or a shooting or some other tragic event, the media always makes note of the necessity of refraining from mentioning the names of the deceased until the *next of kin* can be notified, like the whole thing was circumscribed down to a form or spreadsheet as though— like the clerk on the phone when I was trying to call in a 302—the authorities that be are determined to follow protocol no matter what. I was *next of kin* to Sweetboy. And *they were working on him.* This *work* that they were doing meant that their work could fail, that his life would peter out. The words were meant to prepare me. I was *the next of kin.*

At that point, Jeremiah started praying, *God, please don't let Sweetboy die.* And from there it was a fracas of prayer. Immediately we began to plead—and all I could do was ask for mercy. The Regrets were already crawling up my arms: I let him stay up too late when he was in middle school, I didn't check his homework, sometimes I packed Lunchables instead of healthy food. If only I'd homeschooled him he'd be at home tending to our vegetable garden instead of in the hospital with a breathing tube down his throat.

SEPTIC SHOCK

IT'S BEEN MY PERCEPTION that babies are handed off to parents with a decent-sized bag of guilt tied to their cute little piggy toes; in my mind the bag is gray, black, somewhat ashy, with a consistency that's slightly painful if you pay attention to it. This is how babies enter first light. There are all the jokes about them not coming with instructions and all of that, but maybe the jokes about the need for checklists and directions for the way to put on a diaper are rooted in avoidance. The real burden is the possibility of guilt. It is unfathomable that a parent all of a sudden becomes responsible for a life, how it turns out, another *soul*. This just doesn't make sense.

Guilt is appropriate if you think about it. At least you understand how insufficient you are. Palliating guilt makes it necessary for parents to talk with other parents about failures and find comfort in knowing they're not alone. They, too, used to let their middle schooler stay up too late, or kept the TV on too long when they were young, or got irrationally angry, or gave their child candy in the grocery store to keep them quiet. It's a gift to one another, parents who are honest about these things. But fear is still the backdrop when your child is out of reach, or worry is—fear disfigured.

My own worry when our children were young tended to lean toward the catastrophic. I don't know why. Most people, I think, tend to assume that really bad things only happen to other people, things like cancer and car crashes and maiming and children taken in the middle of the night, but contrary to that, I've always assumed that *I'm* the one who will be maimed or fall into a big dark hole of dust and have to suffer the carnal pains of the world. When I got pregnant with Sophie, I assumed I would miscarry. When I flew in airplanes, I assumed they would crash and my children would be left without a mother. Again, my worries—like when our engine quit as we were driving to DC and surrounded by semi-trucks—had to have rubbed off on Sweetboy. He was a sensitive boy. Which brings me back to guilt.

Of course it's not your fault, someone says even though you suspect they think otherwise. Who would say it's your fault to your face? But then you get hints. You hang back as people talk about how they would never let their kid hang out with So and So. Something bad happens, apart from a child's volition, like sexual abuse, and a parent tells their friend how *they* had decided their child shouldn't go to So and So's house, which implies that they somehow prevented the Bad Thing, which implies that the parents who did let their child go to So and So's house are guilty even though they didn't know So and So molested children.

It took me a long time to understand that sometimes kids do drugs even if their parents follow the rules and check the boxes, and that conversely, kids without healthy upbringings often stay sober and focused. As a young mom I obsessively read all the parenting books. I thought Baumrind's Parenting Typology sounded right—high truth and high grace; high truth refers to high expectations (not to be confused with being demanding and unresponsive), and high grace refers to high affection (not to be confused with being permissive or lenient). But a sandbox on a hot day with tired, fighting kids isn't neat and tidy, and the only way to discover that was to find myself there: exhausted, indecisive, and angry. The books, the whole wheat bread, and the schedule, as they do with any parent, don't happen plenty of times. Things don't always go as planned, and sometimes parenting is about lowering your expectations, or realizing how foolish those expectations were to begin with. I prayed for months that Sophie would get into a certain Ivy League school. I'm ashamed of doing that. What a silly little thing to pray for.

If you're a parent and feel ignorant about drugs, don't be afraid. While Rick and I knew almost nothing about drug abuse or the present drug culture, the atmosphere has since changed and now there's a healthy and robust conversation taking place. Rick and I, perhaps because of our assumption that a certain type of parenting would prevent having a wayward child, were, as the Bible says, caught unawares. But parents today *aren't* caught unawares, and my hope is that our story will both reveal the evil of The Evil, and the magnificence of The Magnificent. And if you're in the midst of a similar story, take comfort in the fact that there are a lot of us out here who understand. There is so much help available now and as complicated as it is; yes, addiction *is* a curable disease.

As we sat in the mauve room with Sweetboy's friends, and eventually our pastor and his wife, I became terrified of the woman in the white coat. Truly terrified. Any moment she could come around the corner because any moment Sweetboy—there in the emergency room where they were *working on him*—could die. The doctors and nurses or whoever was working on him would gently remove the tubes and lines and needles and bags full of liquid from Sweetboy, look at the clock, note the time, and "call it," so that the woman in the white coat would need to come into the room with some kind of compassion on her face and say, "I'm sorry," because what else can they say?

At one point someone had closed the door and it made me hate the room even more. The wall behind the door was scuffed up and dirty and needed to be repainted. There was a small rectangular window above the doorknob, and even though it was smudged and dirty too, I was glad for it. People occasionally walked by, mostly nurses, I could tell by their dark blue scrubs. Sometimes the nurses would be laughing and it widened the separation I felt with the rest of humanity right then because no one in all humanity knew me. I was as unknowable as someone in intense physical pain is unknowable. I think pain, emotional or physical, is always unique; its most muscular tentacle is that it can't be communicated—no one truly understands—so you're left with suction cups at your throat and you can't even ask for a Motrin or a hug it's squeezing so tight. The nurses knew nothing of me or my life and never would. The thin line beneath the door slid in shadows from the hallway activity, slow flickers of gray and white rearranging and reflecting off the glossy floor.

* ✳ *

The nurse didn't say *I'm sorry*, she said *unfortunately*. That one word, *unfortunately*, hung in the air like a Cimmerian creature, some kind of scaly thing with the sole purpose of eating my son.

Two things, I thought, would change my life forever: the compassion on her face, and the word *unfortunately*. *Unfortunately* was a precursor to *he didn't make it*, and a compassionate face meant the woman in the white coat was attempting to soften the blow of telling two parents that they had lost their son. Those are the two things I remember her saying. But then I must have backtracked, because I heard her say, *Unfortunately, he's in septic shock. Do we have your permission to put in a PICC line? It will be a line that goes directly to his heart . . .*

Which meant it was still possible he would live. I didn't care if he had brain damage, or needed to be fed with a spoon, I just wanted his body to be warm. *Oh Lord, please don't let Sweetboy die.*

Rick and I said yes at the same time. *Yes, put the PICC in, whatever, why are you even taking the time to ask us?* And what the hell was septic shock and why was it "unfortunate" he had it? She left and went back through the emergency room doors.

Jeremiah said we should sing. We sang, I don't remember what, just that we did and that it was good. My pastor once said that being in the waiting room catapults yourself into doxology. By "waiting room," he meant of course waiting in general. Waiting and trusting God even when you don't know the outcome. I love how he put it, that waiting "catapults yourself into doxology." Doxology means words or worship or praise, words of glory.

As counterintuitive as it is, for a Christian, words of worship while in that hand-wringing-will-this-ever-end place, can transcend cancer cells, overdoses, and ugly mauve rooms into a foretaste of stars and mountains and a God so beautiful and intimate that you begin to understand the vastness of your future joy. You meet a new joy when you praise God from whom all blessings flow. Back then, though, when I was waiting for news about Sweetboy, I didn't really know these things yet.

The woman in the white coat came in again. "He's stabilized and we're hoping to get him up to the Critical Care Unit as soon as possible . . ."

I said, "So he'll be okay?"

"He's a very sick boy. I'll come let you know when we've moved him up."

He's a very sick boy. More protocol. I wanted to stuff her and her white coat back into the hallway.

Rick got up and went outside. I followed him and we sat at a picnic table and Rick rested his head in his hands and wept. He looked up into the silent, empty blue sky and wailed. I wrapped my arms around him as tight as I could.

We were finally told that Sweetboy had been moved to a room in the CCU so we all crowded into an elevator and headed up. I watched as the numbers above the doors slowly climbed and reminded myself of the most basic of Christian tenets: trust God—it's not a platitude if you say it to yourself. But I couldn't trust him because our son could die. But there was no other option. I thought about what it would be like if Sweetboy died, but then, as though the Holy-Spirit-Bird had just landed on my shoulder, I understood that it would be okay no matter what. However fleeting, at least for that one moment in the elevator, I felt a complete peace.

The waiting room for the CCU had tissue boxes too, only it was surrounded by glass and anyone walking by could see us praying as we sat in brown fabric chairs with wooden armrests. There were two love-seats and three or four small tables. Rick was in the chair next to me with his elbows on his knees praying. There were tri-folded pamphlets resting in small plastic display stands that explained different types of heart failure with pictures of hearts like baby fists, with valves and ventricles and major arteries colored either red or blue depending on which direction the blood traveled. It was hot outside and the Fourth of July was in four days. A handful of flags in our neighborhood were already up.

I wondered whether any of our neighbors knew that our son had overdosed even though I didn't care if they knew, I was just curious. I felt the way women can feel when they're in labor; when the pain gets to that tipping point where you think it can't get any worse, and so you lie there with your legs open and a gaggle of nurses and hopefully the doctor by then, poking around and stretching your vulva and peering at your privates and you couldn't care less if there was nothing but a sliding glass door between you and the outside world, the pain is so bad. I didn't care if our whole neighborhood found out and we got labeled "those" parents, or "that" family. I know this isn't the way a lot of people are, that many parents, rightly so, don't want other people to know what they're going through. For whatever reason I tend to not care about that kind of thing—case in point, I'm writing a book about it.

Sophie was there. I wish now I could go back and hug her. Maybe I did hug her. I was in a haze. I don't remember Neil being there yet but he probably was. I imagine he hung back a bit. I still can't believe he and Sophie had only been married a month and here he was with his new family trying to catch up and figure out what to do to help. Sophie's the one who called Jules in San Francisco to tell her what was happening. She sat with us, she listened as the doctors updated us, she told us to rest and drove us home and back. She stood next to Sweetboy's bed and softly pressed a damp washcloth to his forehead.

Christopher stood up and walked to a small window in the back of the room then came and sat down again. Someone told a joke. I smiled at the joke but didn't laugh. One of my friends showed up and hugged me tight and when we separated she was crying. She said, "I'm sorry," and it made me love her. Even though my mind was still racing I was exhausted; ever since I'd tried to call in the 302 my emotions had been on high alert, and now my bones had turned into what felt like some form of medical rubber. A doctor we hadn't met yet came in, this time a man. He didn't sit down but leaned against the glass wall with his hands behind his back.

"It's still touch and go. He's in septic shock. I've been pumping him with fluids and antibiotics but they don't seem to be doing the trick." Sweetboy seemed like a puzzle he needed to figure out. His mind was on the problem more than us and I wanted it that way, I only wanted him to solve the puzzle; he would have some kind of experimental medicine flown in from a lab in California or somewhere because as a last result experimental medicines flown in from labs in other states always work.

"It's the worst overdose I've seen anyone live through," he said, as though fingering a Rubik's Cube and commenting on how scrambled the colors were. "So far his organs don't seem to be failing, but it's touch and go. His blood pressure is very, very low. I'll keep you updated. There's another med I think I'll try next."

Rick made a phone call to his dad in New York and asked him to come down. He told me later that he'd asked him to come because he knew he couldn't bear to plan Sweetboy's funeral.

Rick went in to see Sweetboy and I hung back, not ready to see him because I didn't know what I would see. He was on life support. Is the worst overdose a doctor has seen anyone live through a good thing or a bad thing? On the one hand he'd used the word *live* and on the other hand he'd used the word *worst*. I kept focusing on singular words and phrases, plucking them out of sentences like the important information was buried inside them. I lined the words up in my head like information I needed to memorize: *Unfortunately, They're working on him, He's a very sick boy, worst, live, It's touch and go, Don't die, Sweetboy, you're my best friend.*

I don't know why I did this, but after Rick left I stood up and went to the back of the room where two Lost Boys I didn't know well were sitting. One of them was a tall kid with long dark hair. He was thin and reminded me of a spider.

"Thanks for helping," I said. He was slumped in his chair, legs out and crossed at the ankles. I think he was wearing black jeans and a black shirt; at least that's what I remember.

He tucked one side of his hair behind an ear and the rest hung down and covered the other side of his face. He spoke quietly, almost a whisper, "I could've done more."

"Well thanks anyway," I said, then asked, "What should we do if he gets better?" I don't know why I asked him this. I barely knew the kid. Maybe I thought he had some hard-earned knowledge that he could pass on to us. Maybe he'd seen the The Evil and knew how to fight in the context of crumbling curbs and broken glass windows. Maybe he knew how to fling syringes like darts into heroin's sides.

I'll never forget what he said: "You can stop buying him cigarettes."

And we *had* bought them for him. We, two educated, non-ignorant parents, had habitually bought our son cigarettes. We justified it thinking it would keep him from harder drugs, that it would keep him from being anxious, that it would make him happy, and all we wanted was for him to be happy. However, supplying him with cigarettes only made it easier for him to get heroin. Cigarettes are expensive and we were taking care of him in a way that we shouldn't have been taking care of him. We knew exactly what enabling was, and yet we still did it.

His words stung like I'd just yanked the intubation tube from Sweetboy's trachea and stuck in a cigarette.

* * *

Sophie was standing next to his bed with her hand resting on his shoulder. A clear canister the size of a coffee can slowly filling with thick black fluid coming from his lungs hung from a hook on the wall. The canister was over halfway full and a nurse came in and made a note of it. There was an enormous sliding glass door and a standing desk in the hallway next to the room with two computer screens and papers filled with notations taped to the wall above them. A curtain was slid halfway across the sliding door. A urine bag with measurements— 200mL, 300mL—was attached to the foot of Sweetboy's bed, and the nurse lifted it and made a note of that too. Blue plastic sleeves were wrapped around his legs and every few minutes a low growl-like hum caused them to slowly inflate like a congested inhale before they relaxed again and the air seeped back out, making a clicking sound as it did.

A monitor next to his bed never stopped beeping. There were square white stickers and wires covering his chest and needles taped on his arms and lines seemed to be trailing over his entire body. Near his left shoulder was a port that had some kind of medical plug adapter that pumped him with liquid, I assumed it was the PICC line to his heart. There were so many monitors in his room and so many numbers and lines and carefully measured sounds indicating a still pumping heart or brain function or pulse or inside bodily thing I didn't know existed, that the room felt robotic. It was still hard to see his face hidden under the intubation tube and tape. Sophie brushed his hair off his forehead and Rick sat next to him praying. I cried softly.

I prayed and I cried and fingered wadded up tissues and blew snot from my nose and made half jokes in between for sanity. One of our friends came and leaned over his bed and held his face in her hands and prayed for a long time in what sounded like another language.

* * *

We went back to the waiting room and Rick tried to update everyone even though there wasn't much to say. There was one guy, the husband of a friend, who seemed particularly compassionate and I asked him if he wanted to see Sweetboy. It's strange, but I briefly felt proud when I asked him. I think now it was because only Rick and I had the authority to allow or not allow someone to see Sweetboy. Only we decided who went through those wide double doors to the CCU that only opened if a nurse buzzed you in. It was *my* boy who was asleep with hoses keeping him alive and no one could touch him unless I said they could touch him. I was in control like I was in control when I was ripping cushions off the couch in The Chill Spot.

He said yes, and I asked a nurse to let him in. Rick and I stayed in the waiting room, knee to knee with some of our friends. I thought about the possibility that Sweetboy, like a bomb finally exploding, could have a code black or code blue while Rick and I were gone and we wouldn't see the people in the scrubs running to his room and paddling him back and then losing him and then paddling him back and then losing him. If he died, would he know whether we were with him? Later, my friend's husband told me that seeing him had been hard, that it didn't look like Sweetboy and that seeing him had affected him.

The doctor came out again and leaned against the wall again and again said it was "touch and go." I asked him what we should pray for and he told us we could pray that his blood pressure would come up so we did. "His blood pressure is very low," he said more than once. "I'm having a cardiologist assess things because his heartbeat is very weak." Code blue. Code black. We needed to get back to his room. Everyone in the waiting room prayed that his blood pressure would come up. The physician told me later that at that point his heart was only beating fourteen times a minute. Someone told me to go home and take a bath. *Go home and take a bath, you'll feel better.* Someone else told me to go home and take a shower. Apparently, you don't feel anxious if you're clean. The hell if I'm going to go home and take a bath, *you* go home and take a bath. I'm staying for the bomb and the paddles.

BACKSTORY

It was because of The Lost Boys that Sweetboy didn't die in the pool house. I didn't know it until much later, but after he took off in his Subaru, or even before that, perhaps when I saw the text on his phone, a chain of events had begun that ended up keeping him alive until the paramedics got there. In retrospect, the events were like a necklace of pearls you follow backwards until they reveal the start that determines the ending. Guy wakes up on 9/11, heads off for the subway, realizes he forgot his briefcase, goes home to get it, planes hit while he's home getting his briefcase, and thus God is good, never mind the rest of the three thousand plus people who died.

But even though far more than three thousand people have died from heroin overdoses, I kept trusting God because if I didn't believe in God everything was only random, and I knew—perhaps especially when I was in that elevator looking at the climbing numbers and felt that moment of complete peace—that there was purpose in all that was happening, and, although in a vague and yet to be proven way, I believed this even if Sweetboy were to die. I don't know anything about why God allows this or that horrible thing, but I do know that God isn't a synthetic God, and that there are stories of angles and visions sans acid, and *a man in Christ who fourteen years ago was caught up to the third heaven.*

* ✱ *

The events that prevented Sweetboy from dying began when he took off in his Subaru.

That's about when Jeremiah, who was spending a few days camping out at some kind of Christian version of Burning Man in the middle of Pennsylvania, thought maybe it would be a good idea if he went home early. He was enjoying himself, but for some reason he felt uneasy and decided to come home.

Sweetboy, after taking off in his car, had driven to the other side of town. I don't know how long it took him to decide to go to The Badlands or if it took any time at all—I imagine he was already beginning to experience the sweats and the itches that go with withdrawal. He did have the good sense to look for someone to go with him. I think he got a few nos before someone, I'm not sure who, said he'd go with him to make sure he was safe. (Eventually, after Sweetboy was in the

CCU, the cops searched his car and found the usual opiatic paraphernalia but only tossed it. Perhaps they did this because it was his first offense. They could have thrown him in prison, which in some cases can be a good thing, but there's also a fairly well-known cycle of prison-parole-rehab-prison-parole-rehab that, like a cancer in remission that always returns, screws up many lives. I'm still grateful for whatever police were on duty the morning he wouldn't wake up. The night the cop stopped him on his way to The Badlands and this time, when they threw his needles and empty bags away rather than arresting him, I believe ultimately protected him. Knowing Sweetboy, I think prison would have made things far worse and would have exacerbated some of the issues that likely played a part in his becoming addicted to heroin to begin with. Sweetboy was given second chances that other kids don't always get. He was a clean looking white boy; he came from a quaint, middle class neighborhood. His car might as well have had a bumper sticker on it that said "Eat Local." In a way the cop that stopped him on his way to Philly saved my son's life. And Jeremiah saved his life, too, as well as Christopher, Sam, and even though he was out of town, Stephan too.)

In The Badlands Sweetboy bought a bundle: ten bags of heroin. He shot up even before he returned from the city, and the boy he was with—knowing he was in danger—threw away whatever Sweetboy didn't have on him. People were hanging out drinking at Christopher and Sam's. They lived down the street from Danny, the boy with the pool house. I asked Christopher what he remembers about that night and this is what he told me:

"Sweetboy kept using throughout the night. There was even conversation and concern about his current and mental state. It was a long night with a decent amount of people staying over. By the end of the night, Sweetboy was visibly in rough shape and it seemed prudent that he had some space to recuperate without watchful eyes. Danny was heading back up to his house and Sweetboy was (allowed or assigned?) to stay in the pool house. Sam helped him get settled up there, but was worried and noticed something wasn't right. He stayed up there with him through the night, while we went to sleep."

* * *

"I cannot remember the time but it was certainly morning because it was light out when I woke up to Sam rushing into my room in a panic. He told me I needed to come up to help; Sweetboy wasn't doing well. I woke up Jeremiah, who was asleep on the couch, on my way out of the house. We arrived at the pool house where Sweetboy was lying there wheezing and choking on his own vomit. His face was discolored and unresponsive. I turned him on his side and tried to clear his throat by pulling the vomit out of his mouth as he wheezed. His face was turning more blue and purple as he continued to suffocate on more of his own vomit. I can still hear the sound when I think about it. There was no positive change in his state and as the severity of the situation sunk in I think Sam left to tell Danny's parents. I cannot remember who called 911. I believe it was Danny's mom. The experience was so traumatic and jarring that I cannot remember the order of the chaos that ensued with the arrival of Danny's parents, the medics, and you and Rick."

* * *

I don't know when it was that he called me. Maybe he called from the pool house, or right after he shot up in his car, or maybe while he was stumbling to the pool house. I wonder what precedes an opiate overdose, what precedes the blue-gray that precedes death. Is it when they fall asleep? Nod off? Are they just all over listless?

It was a beautiful summer night, crisp and clear. There had to have been stars. Rick and I were on the other side of town in our living room catching up with Sophie and Neil even as I couldn't stop thinking about the cop at our door and Sweetboy peeling out of the driveway hours earlier. I tried not to look at my phone too often even though I knew Sweetboy didn't have his phone and wouldn't be able to call. We should have let him keep his phone; *what were we thinking?* Sweetboy would shoot up, maybe with heroin cut with fentanyl or Drano or whatever dealers were cutting it with at the time, and probably die, or never come back and disappear into some other universe the way I imagine purgatory, if I believed in it, would be like. Some flat, earthless place without dark and without light.

But even as my mind wandered to my own personal versions of recremental filth, on the other side of town Sweetboy's best friends were praying for him. Sam decided to sit with Sweetboy in the pool house, lay down on the grass, stared at the sky, and prayed for him. Christopher, Jeremiah, and Sam; I don't know if anyone else was there. I think about that moment a lot, I imagine them lying on the grass and staring up at the stars, all three of them lined up with their hands behind their heads and their elbows almost touching.

I can see the yard; I picture Christopher and Sam's house. There are four brothers total, entirely different from one another and yet profoundly similar, as though when they played kick the can as boys, the tinny pings of the can on the asphalt lodged in their ears and stuck, giving them the same late summer evening background noise that would be with them throughout their lives. When I used to drop Sweetboy off at their house before he could drive, it seemed so obvious to me that it was a house of boys. There were a couple small decorative floral flags along the front walk and some planters near the door, but they appeared to be only nods to their mother; everything else bloomed male—a rarely used basketball hoop with tufts of unmowed grass at its base, sports stickers on one of the upstairs windows. There was a soft, almost indecipherable wornness encircling the house. The front lawn was treeless except for a few overgrown bushes, and it sloped slightly down toward the road. I imagine every prepubescent voice innocent and hollow as those aluminum cans floating over that house and neighborhood, then gently sinking as they start to fill with truth. There are things that speed up maturity like a train skipping a stop and that night—even as Sweetboy's central nervous system was starting to shut down—those boys leapt a couple yards closer to wisdom. Even now, when I think of them lying in the grass praying for Sweetboy, it gives me a retroactive wonder.

The next morning it was Sam who couldn't wake him up, and it was Jeremiah who called us, and it was Sophie who sped us across town to where my legs turned to wax and I crumpled to the ground after seeing him gray-blue. That grass, that crisp summer night, that prayer. He would have been dead in a matter of minutes if Sam wasn't with him. That's what the cardiologist told us. The police told us that too.

Everything that happened that night contributed to him not dying in that pool house. Christopher, Sam, Jeremiah; if any of you are reading this, thank you for lying on the grass and praying, thank you for sitting with him through the night, thank you for coming home from Christian Burning Man. Death was like a paused fuse. That night was full of tiny wires like dendrites, tips close enough to spark across a mortal gap but blocked by a tacit faith.

* * *

The philosopher Dallas Willard in *The Divine Conspiracy*, says, "If you have a friend who is addicted to heroin or lost in the jungles of intellectual faddishness, then whatever else you may do to help him, you had better pray." Willard goes on to say that we should pray, not just because fixing him is beyond us, but because it's good that fixing him is beyond us.

Near the end of the Gospel of Luke, Jesus tells Peter he will deny him. Jesus knows this will happen, and could have "fixed" Peter, but chooses not to because fixing him would not have allowed for the difficult circumstances that ultimately shaped Peter's faith. While The Lost Boys were on the other side of town lying in the grass and praying for Sweetboy, Sweetboy knew nothing of what was happening, but he was being prayed for. Many times I drew great encouragement in knowing that God could use all of the awfulness, like he did with Peter, to grow Sweetboy's faith. And not only his faith, but The Lost Boys' as well; and my own faith, it would grow my faith too.

When Christ prayed for Peter, it was with Peter's growth in mind. Willard writes:

> Jesus said to Peter, with sadness perhaps, but with great confidence in the Father, "I have requested, concerning you, that your faith might not die. And when you have straightened up, uphold your brothers" (Luke 22:32). I think there is perhaps no other scene in all scripture that so forcefully illustrates the community of prayerful love as this response to Peter. He used no condemnation, no shame, no "pearls of wisdom" on him. And he didn't use supernatural power to rewire his soul or his brain. It was just this: "I have requested, concerning you, that your faith might not die." And it corresponds perfectly to Matthew 7:1-11. It is Jesus' beautiful pattern for us to practice in our relationships to those close to us.

✳ ✳ ✳

I don't know if Dallas Willard loved someone addicted to heroin, but he knew the crucible; he understood how things proceed. Those two most difficult barriers to get through: coming to peace with the fact that fixing them is beyond you and understanding that it's good that it's beyond you.

ELEVATORS ALL
THE WAY DOWN

I'VE NEVER FIGURED out where those hospital smells come from— the salty uneaten ham sitting on trays in the hallways? Some uber-chlorinated cleaner with enough antibiotic strength to kill atavistic microbes? No matter, it was always there and I was never able to ignore it when I got off the elevators in the CCU. And the smell grew stronger when I was buzzed through the double doors that only I could enter that opened to the sterilized blue hallway lined with glass doors and patients in beds that looked like intubated shrouds covered in white sheets.

Sometimes I wonder where the patients go when their heart monitor rejects them and the intubation tubes don't matter anymore. Where are the bodies sent? They must end up in the basement in some stainless steel room where they're sliced open like melons so patholo-gists can dig around in blood-pulp to confirm whatever reason for death was noted on a form that was probably attached to one of their dead toes. Or maybe the tagged toes are only in the movies. They probably have a seemingly more appropriate way of identifying them now. Then of course there are the drawers. Waylen, after he died, was moved to a room before he went to the morgue. I know, because that's where Stephan sat praying for him. But what about when someone in the CCU dies? When loved ones have already said their goodbyes and a body needs to be moved to the morgue? I'm sure there's some kind of janitorial elevator the orderlies use. I think about the orderlies who have the job of taking bodies to the morgue. What do they think about while they're moving them? Can they go about their days like anyone else does when their job is to move dead people? Does the brevity of life strike them as they stand next to the dead, maybe a little irritated that they have to wait longer for their lunch break, and watch the numbers descending above the elevator doors just as I watched them ascend so I could stand next to the bed of my still-alive son? Are those orderlies the sorts of people who compartmentalize things, leave their thoughts when they leave the hospital? If Sweetboy died he would need to be wheeled down the hall with a sheet over his face. I was ter- rified of this—or fascinated in a terrified way. I think sometimes when we fear certain things we become strangely fascinated by them even as our arms and chests might tingle and our bones turn to medical rubber, like someone afraid of sharks that can't keep their eyes off the special on TV that shows gruesome attacks over and over. We peer timidly around corners, we seek out some kind of strange confirmation that our fears aren't founded on nothing. Maybe the salty ham or chlori- nated cleaner can still be smelled as the dead are descending to the basement in the special elevators the size of small bedrooms that pass the maternity wards and surgery floors as they fall, the odor of those places leaking into the lifts through narrow cracks and separations of elevator steel.

The first time we entered the CCU the smell was mildly pungent. From that moment on it always got to me. There wasn't a time when I went through those double doors and wasn't surprised by it. I won- dered if other people were as struck by it as I was, or if for me it was more than an odor, if the smells reminded me of Sweetboy's body failing. But there were always people in the waiting room to pray with or talk to, and that usually helped me stop thinking about the smell.

The doctor didn't know if there was brain activity. Sweetboy had been significantly deprived of oxygen.

Someone was always passing me Kleenex and I kept telling lame jokes. Rick and I have always made jokes in woolly situations like we're taking swigs of tequila that renders what surrounds us inconsequential.

"So I guess Harvard is out of the question," I said, fingering a wad of pressed together Kleenex, and a few people laughed. The truth is, even though I asked for specifics from the doctors and sometimes looked up medical abstracts, I *wanted* nebulous answers. I didn't want to know the truth because the truth terrified me.

Jeremiah said we should pray that his brain would be okay.

But even if he did have brain damage his body would still be warm and I could hug him. I've heard people say when a loved one dies, *if only I could hug him one more time*. Of course if you had "one more time" you'd want another "one more time." It's a Catch-22, always putting off the inevitable.

* * *

When Sweetboy was almost two, every night he would sit on my lap and without fail I would read an Eric Carle book to him—*The Very Hungry Caterpillar*. It's full of colorful collages and begins with how hungry the caterpillar is and then you turn the page and there's a line of different types of food, sweet things like candy and cakes, and whenever I got to that page he would pretend to grab each one of them and gobble them up. And then on the next page it says, "The next day was Sunday again. The caterpillar ate through a nice green leaf, and after that he felt much better." So the caterpillar eats a healthy leaf and feels better and makes a cocoon, and then as you turn to the very last page there's a beautiful, colorful butterfly that takes up both pages and it's almost shocking to be reminded of the beauty of a butterfly. Every time I got to that last page I got a little choked up.

* ✳ *

James Baldwin quotes the Bible in his short story *Sonny's Blues*. The first time I read that story, when I got to the last sentence, I felt like a great hot wind had smashed into my chest. There's a place where Baldwin, referring to heroin, writes the words . . . *ice in the veins and have it never let up.* Even though Baldwin uses ice as a metaphor to describe heroin, I think of heroin as a warm thing. I think it's the mothers who feel like they have ice in their veins. Heroin is warm for the user, but feels like ice to those who love them. The last sentence in *Sonny's Blues*, the one that feels to me like hot wind, is referring to a drink of milk and scotch—a *cup of trembling*, Baldwin calls it, and it sits on a piano and shudders with the music while a heroin addict plays.

In the book of Zechariah the *cup of trembling* is Jerusalem, but for Baldwin—and for me—it's heroin and everything that comes with it. A drink of milk and scotch is just about right. Addicts, I've found, can be particularly nostalgic. They want to be five again, sitting at the kitchen table and drinking the milk, but the scotch is necessary for the zing. Without the scotch, the milk can make you gag.

At one point Rick and I had gone home to rest, and I stood in the shower and cried. Showers are a great place to cry because the water hitting your shoulders and face make the tears seem less potent, like they're right at home, the faintly salty wetness could just as well be nothing but the water from the showerhead, so in a way it's like you're not crying at all. The only reason you still know you are is because of how your heart hurts and your face is half scrunched up the way it is when you have a good hard cry that makes you feel a little bit better. And then the warmth of the water gives you comfort the way being under a thick blanket on a cold night gives you comfort. You don't ever have to leave, you can stay under that blanket until the outside world is warm again. When I was crying in the shower I felt like I could just stay there until everything would be okay again. And when you're crying in the shower no one can hear you except maybe when you find yourself making an audible involuntary suck to get more air. When I was in the shower crying I didn't think anyone could hear me, but I guess I needed to get more air now and again because Rick heard me.

Many men seem to have an impenetrable emotional membrane, something that has probably provided the expedience needed to keep spearing each other with bayonets or machine-gunning each other to death in wartime, and yet I think it can backfire so that they find themselves with truncated emotions, however utilitarian, during a thick muck of bloody heartache.

If like Adam in the garden, Rick's given me one of his ribs, he's just as strong without it. He made decisions while I was functioning as logically as a June beetle smacking a window. Rick was strong when we thought we were saying goodbye to Sweetboy, when we thought that he would never wake up, just fade away from us not knowing how intense our love for him was. I don't know why I felt that way, that he wouldn't know how much we loved him if we couldn't tell him we loved him one last time. He did know of course; he had always known. Love is not only full of power and can change things, it's also funny, and by that I mean ironic. It makes no sense. We often want to say, "I love you" most earnestly when a loved one has done something that hurts us. Suicide might be the best example of this; even though you've been wounded by someone, you desperately want them to know you love them. Or perhaps when a parent leaves and a kid just wants to have them back so he can tell them he loves them. I wanted to tell Sweetboy

I loved him. I did tell him of course, in his ear, as I gently moved one of the many lines attached to his body aside and tried to ignore the tube snaking down his throat. But I wanted his eyes open and the words repeated to me. How odd the words *I love you* are. We say other things over and over again, like "You're beautiful" but then in a way "You're beautiful" is just another take on "I love you." Why do we keep saying it? The words should have become meaningless by now, but we keep at it because they aren't, so I guess they never will be.

Rick loved me without saying the words. He stayed with Sweetboy through the night so I could go home and sleep. He was with him when, like an alien thing, he jerked and sweated through withdrawals. The next morning Rick told me he understood now why people refer to withdrawals as kicking the habit because Sweetboy was kicking all over the place. I imagined them having to tie him down. Maybe they did—Rick didn't tell me the particulars, only that it was a good thing I wasn't there. I'm sure he was vomiting and pooping yellow because that's what happens when an addict quits cold turkey.

The morning after Rick sat with Sweetboy and watched him kick the habit Rick looked more tired than I'd ever seen him.

When he heard me crying in the shower, I gathered myself together and dried off. I took a towel and made a large swipe on the mirror so I could see my face before it fogged up again. I had to wipe the mirror a few times to get a good look because I wanted to make sure my eyes weren't too swollen, but even after taking a cold washcloth and pressing it to my eyes, it was still obvious I'd been crying. When I came out Rick was lying on the bed with his hands behind his head, so I went straight to the closet to rummage around until my eyes looked better. But it didn't matter, because he said, "Keep crying. Cry for both of us."

There were three times when I glimpsed the depth of my husband's pain. One was when he lay on top of Sweetboy and told him not to die because he was his best friend. Another was when he sat at the picnic table and wailed. And this one, when I came out of the shower and he told me to cry for both of us.

TEN TO
THIRTY PERCENT

HEARTS DON'T BREAK. They swell and pop. I think that might be what happened to Jesus' heart when he died. The Bible says that when he was on the cross and the soldiers pierced him in the side, water and blood gushed out, which likely was a pericardial effusion, a buildup of pericardial fluid. Like a buffer of water, pericardial fluid surrounds the heart and protects it and when there is effusion, the fluid can also contain blood. It's easy to access medical abstracts online. Sometimes there are shadowy scans and images of internal organs and I'd bring my computer screen close to see clearly the darkened arteries and layers of foggy white tissue. I wanted to know as much as I could about Sweetboy's condition—the more medical information I could get my hands on, the better. Like a passenger learning to fly a plane with an unconscious pilot, I tried to inhale a medical degree in a matter of days.

There's a condition called broken heart syndrome. It's also called takotsubo cardiomyopathy and happens when there's severe physical or emotional stress, and Jesus' heart was nothing if not emotionally stressed. (In Gethsemane, the night before he was crucified, he was so distraught he sweat blood.) With broken heart syndrome, the heart weakens in actual sorrow and the left ventricle begins to bulge, which can cause pericardial effusion and at times even myocardial rupture, which is just what it sounds like—a burst heart. A loved one dies; a spouse, or a child, and the heart bloats with grief. A broken heart doesn't crack down the middle, it swells, leaks, and ruptures.

When he was in the CCU, Sweetboy had broken heart syndrome. The first time I heard about it was when the cardiologist—still working to figure out what was going on—suggested that he might have it and that it could have something to do with his low blood pressure. That's when he told us his heart was beating fourteen times a minute and that he'd never seen anything like that before. Sweetboy lay unconscious, his heart swollen and barely beating while he was wheeled down to scans and x-rays and MRIs so radiologists could stare at the white ghosts of his organs on screens and speculate. Like a balloon squeezed so that the air is forced to one side, his left ventricle bloated and his heart swelled fragile, which set off a chain of events that swelled left ventricles all over the Philadelphia area and then the world. Rick called Stephan, who was in Florida, to ask him to pray, and Stephan called his dad, and his dad was in the Philippines speaking at a conference for pastors and they stopped everything and prayed. Social media spun tides of welter the day my son's heart was swollen and barely beating. Mothers prayed. Fathers prayed. The Lost Boys prayed. We held each other's hands and bent over in prayer like so many stalks in earth's planetary winds.

* * *

Sweetboy's face, although pale, had color, but his toes were cold. He was being pumped with so much fluid the bags hanging from monitors seemed to go flat every fifteen minutes. Someone was always coming in to change a bag, and every time someone came in to change a bag, I looked hopefully at their face, as though I'd see an expression of some sort—like a thumbs up or a thumbs down that indicated "good prognosis" or "bad prognosis." Whatever was in the fluid was supposed to increase his blood pressure but still nothing was working. The cardiologist, at least twice, came in and told us that other than his heart, so far there was no sign of organ failure. With sepsis, multiple organ failure can be like a cascade; organ after organ fails and it's almost impossible to reverse. The plastic container shaped like a coffee can that hung from the wall kept filling with black fluid. Was this good or bad?

Rick and I were sitting quietly next to his bed and heard a nurse in the hallway telling Jeremiah that he couldn't come in. A few moments later Jeremiah peeked his head around the corner—"We love you, Sweetboy!" he yelled—and went back to the waiting room.

The cardiologist was talkative about how he was trying to bring up Sweetboy's blood pressure and get his heart rate up. They kept wheeling him out for what I assumed were more scans, his room left empty, tubes wrapped around monitors and IV fluids left hanging on their singular designated scaffolds halfway up to the ceiling. Rick and I would go out to the waiting room and sit with our friends until they wheeled him back.

There's an article, "Sepsis and the Heart," by M. Jeremiah, M. W. Merx, and C. Weber, that says the presence of cardiovascular dysfunction in sepsis is associated with a significantly increased mortality rate of 70 percent to 90 percent compared with 20 percent in septic patients without cardiovascular impairment. Sweetboy had sepsis and cardiovascular impairment and low blood pressure and his heart was beating fourteen times a minute. At that point his chance of survival was 10 to 30 percent.

One day recently, when I was picking up some groceries, I heard a boy yell to his brother, "Jose, look how close we are. Jose, Jose, look how close we are!"

GLORY'S IN THE FRONT YARD

RICK THINKS ONE REASON we don't see miracles is that we aren't on the frontlines yanking people out of foxholes. He says that if you are, if you have the bullets pinging and the grenades booming, you know how much you need God and you know he's the only one who can help. Rick says we don't bother to pray because we assume we don't need God.

I think The Evil does his best to turn up the volume of "Sympathy for the Devil" so we don't think God is anywhere even when an angel wearing a super white shirt is walking around your front yard and stops and looks up at your son's window.

It wasn't until months later that Rick told me about the angel because he says for some reason it was a private thing and he didn't even want to tell me. He still doesn't talk about it. Rick had come home for a few hours and was in the dining room praying—we were taking turns at the hospital so we could each get some rest, mostly because we were told to do this, not because either of us could actually rest. That's when he saw the man in the glowing white T-shirt.

When Rick finally did tell me about it, I imagined the shirt like a Fruit-of-the-Loom T-shirt because that's the kind of incidental my visual brain goes to. All Rick actually said was that the shirt was white. That's the first thing he told me, that he saw a man wearing a very white shirt, as though the whole point of what he saw was that the man was wearing a white shirt. Super white. Pure white. In the book of Psalms it says one day we will be white as snow, which is cool because many snowflakes pressed together are what makes snow white, and as most of us learned in grade school, not one snowflake is like another. In the

Gospel of Mark, when Jesus is standing on a mountain, transfigured, it says his clothes were exceedingly white such as no launderer on earth can whiten them.

Rick was in the dining room praying when he looked out the window and saw the man in the white shirt walking in the front yard. Then the man stopped and looked up at Sweetboy's dormered window. I imagine him shielding his eyes in the early July sun. Rick said at first he thought it was Neil, but that didn't make sense because at that point he had gone back to work in DC. It wasn't until the man had disappeared that Rick understood that it was an angel, and he says it wasn't "*maybe* that was an angel," but *that was an angel*. It was just a fact. There's a place in the Bible that says after Jesus was crucified some of his followers were on the road to Emmaus, talking to a stranger, and it wasn't until the man was gone that they realized it was Jesus. Like Jesus' followers on the road to Emmaus, it was only after the angel left that Rick understood what he'd seen. After the man was gone Rick knew it had been an angel and that the angel had been looking up at Sweetboy's room. Was the angel deciding what to do? Did God tell the angel to make sure Sweetboy didn't die? Is that what he was doing?

* * *

A physician wearing suit pants and a crisp white shirt—you could see the soft lines where the material had been folded—came in to give us an update. I had my latest balled up Kleenex in my hands but wasn't crying. He told us Sweetboy was still in septic shock and we'd need to see how things would go, that the next twenty-four hours were crucial. Rick asked what we should pray for. He said, "Pray his blood pressure will come up," so we kept praying his blood pressure would come up.

Every time I went to his room to sit with him I felt better. There have probably been studies done on what colors are the most comforting or cheery, what colors are best for promoting healing, in hospital rooms. The walls in his rooms were painted a faint light blue. Almost white.

The next morning the same doctor came in and told us he was encouraged, his blood pressure was going up, and he was going to wheel him down for another CAT scan to see how his heart was. He was doing much better, but "wasn't out of the woods quite yet." I hated that phrase like I hated "next of kin," but I liked the word *quite*. *Quite* was a hopeful word. If you compare *not out of the woods yet*, with *not out of the woods quite yet*, the latter sounds much better.

The 10- to 30-percent chance that he would live went up to a 30- to 50-percent chance he would live. A nurse came in while we were sitting next to Sweetboy and we told her we'd been praying. "It's working," she smiled and said, "His blood pressure's coming up," and replaced an IV bag before leaving.

THE THINGS THEY CARRY

THERE'S A FAMILY that lived up the street from me when I was growing up. I remember playing in their backyard and the youngest, a boy around six or seven, would sit on a swing, his feet stationary in the dirt, his knees the axis for the slow circular movements of the swing, and he'd whisper to himself some kind of Euclidean geometry. His parents were physicists and his brain seemed full of numbers I would never understand.

The differences of families. There are families with super–taste buds that eat sea creatures for dinner, their kids eager for one more bite, and families with mental illness, and families with inherited heart defects, and circus families that go back generations, when their peculiarities could gather a return and sustain a certain way of life: vertebrae with the ability to bend back onto themselves, an uncanny knack for balancing large objects on pinky fingers, overly tall, lanky bodies, or the opposite: tiny people with tiny feet and tiny hands and squeaky voices to boot. Families that could prophesy, raise a table with the palms of their hands, lift their faces toward the gods, and utter cursory things in a profound way: *twelve years minus five and a new individual will come into your life . . .*

The difference of souls. We look sideways at each other and compare even though comparing is illogical. Our diseases are custom-made like our souls are custom-made and we inherit them along with our double-jointed elbows and savant-like math skills—things are nature and things are nurture and never shall the two divide. And whether you're raised in a carnival or study at MIT, you can still break an ankle or need a root canal and end up with a bottle of hard-to-resist Vicodin on your bedside table.

It took a while for me grasp how incomprehensible and complex the factors are that lead to addiction. If I'd had a tablespoon of cherry-flavored medicine that heals all ills, and I could have slipped it into the mouth of every struggling kid I knew I would have, but that's not the way addiction works. There's no single way to cure all. And there is nothing and no one to pin the responsibility of addiction entirely on—no sister or brother or friend, no mother or father—all of us carry things, hurt ankles and hurt hearts, and the only real cherry-flavored medicine is love, which of course we all need—sober or not. Understanding that addiction is a disease with many causes and without a comprehensive cure has a way of draining the judgment right out of you.

There were the kids that hung out in our living room with Rick and ate brownies in the kitchen with me and stayed in our home and had parents I talked with on the phone and parents I prayed with, kids who knew the love of family and friends, kids who stayed here and kids who didn't, kids I didn't know but prayed for, kids far away and kids standing next to me. I'll list them so you can practice not judging. Practice not blaming. Think of each one of them and love them from a distance and practice not judging because, regardless of why, they carried heavy burdens.

There was the girl who sat next to the wall in our living room trying to stay awake while Rick led a Bible study, then nodded off as she flaked out and gave in to the opiates seeping around every blood-corner of every organ in her body, and the kid with the pastor father who messed up and messed up again and finally came around, and the kid who smoked weed because it was the only way he could sleep. There was the kid whose parents kidnapped her and dropped her off at a camp for untoward teenagers so she'd finally figure out life, and the kid who hated his parents, and the kid who didn't, the kid who stole beer from garages and the kid who drank Imodium to get high, and the other kid who drank hand sanitizer in rehab so he could suck as much alcohol as possible from it and hopefully feel a little bit less anxious but ended up on the bathroom floor with severe pancreatitis before he finally got sober. There's the kid who went away for a year to a rehab on a beautiful mountain and sang songs to Jesus and saw rainbows when he really needed the encouragement of seeing a rainbow, and came home but couldn't resist another needle, *just one more needle and then I'll be done.* There was the kid who made his way across America visiting rehab after rehab and then would phone his parents asking for more money for clothes or food and use it for meth instead and then end up on a street in California where his mother finally found him and could barely recognize him he was so dirty and half-alive so that she held his head in her lap in the back seat of a car as they drove to another rehab which would work for sure, this one would. There's the kid who did psychedelics until his eyes glassed over and he became terrified of the people trying to get him—the government or something was after him—so Rick asked him to mow the lawn because then maybe he'd think about something other than the government trying to get him and he mowed the lawn in spirals, like a thumbprint that matched his own mind. There was the skinny kid who smoked copious amounts of weed whom I've always loved so much who couldn't get enough of his Bible, who loved his Bible until he couldn't stop turning pages, reading too much into individual words and then saw the eyes of his friends speaking to him without words, like blue eyes said one thing and brown eyes said another, and ended up in a psychiatric ward, so that Sweetboy visited him to cheer him up while his mother and I prayed, only I didn't pray for him as much as she did because she loved him, as parents say these days, "to the moon and back." And there's the kid who took Vivitrol for months so he'd stop using heroin because he wanted to stop using heroin, but if you use heroin after not using it for months you can die quickly; and he did use it, and he did die. The Vivitrol and Suboxone and Seroquel and Lamictal are burdens in themselves, but worth it if they help you quit the heroin. There was the kid who didn't use heroin, but felt his body begin to freeze up and his heart pound fierce in his chest so that he went to Rick's side of the bed in the middle of the night, kneeled down, and asked us to pray for him. There was the track-star kid I didn't like much because he'd insulted one of Jules's friends—and it must have been quite an insult because Jules punched him in the face even though she isn't the kind of person who punches people in the face. He moved to the Bronx and made money in Manhattan by selling art and selling drugs until he messed with the wrong people and then they messed with him and he disappeared so that we all followed Facebook posts about him and felt sorry for his parents and wondered where he could be, until he showed up back in the Bronx in a downstairs club late at night dead, as they say, with a bullet through his head. Rick once asked how bad the clubs in Philly were and Sweetboy told him he'd once seen a girl who led her boyfriend around on a leash. There was also a kid who overdosed on the dance floor so that paramedics had to revive him and carry him out on a stretcher. I've always wondered if the people kept dancing, trying not to kick him in the face as he lay unconscious. There was the kid who prayed all the time and the other kid who prayed with him and the kid who went to an island somewhere with a group of Christians who spoke in tongues until it weirded him out and he came home so that he could figure things out for himself and then left for somewhere again and speared fish in the ocean and helped the people who lived there because he loves his God and he has a knack for spearing fish and building people houses. He's the one who drywalled The Chill Spot and built me a compost bin. There was the really smart kid who finally felt Jesus go from his head to his heart while Sweetboy lay unconscious, the same kid, Sweetboy's best friend, who Rick pulled aside in the CCU so he could hug him for what felt like forever and tell him that he needed to hug him because he was Sweetboy's best friend and it was as close as he could get to hugging his own son. There was Stephan's friend, the kid I talked to in the kitchen for a long time about how Jesus felt the same burdens as us when he was on the cross, only an infinity of them, so that our own burdens will be lifted and he will carry them for us and he cried he was so struck by the wonder of it—that same kid who, one day later, drank too much and flipped his car and died, so that Rick and I went to the funeral and watched as his friend who had been in the car with him limped to his casket to say goodbye even though he had a shaved head and a band of staples from ear to ear that we were all having a hard time not looking at. And there was the mother of the kid who died in the car that flipped, saying over and over *give the boy a seat* at his funeral because life didn't make much sense at that point and she probably didn't know what else to say. There were the two kids who tasted the love of Christ and loved him back so they went to college to learn more. And another kid who was doing heroin who ended up walking down Route 3 with her suitcase after her parents made her leave, so that her parents half laughed even as they were crying, it was such a sight, but then her parents loved her something crazy so we met every week to pray for her and now her face lights up and she loves freedom and has a personality that will cheer anyone who's with her. There's the kid in jail for trying to stab someone with the needle of a syringe, at least that's the story. There's that kid who went to jail, got out, used again, and drove his car over a woman so that she almost died and still the woman forgave him but he shot heroin *one last time* and then died anyway. There were those kids who prayed over and over for Sweetboy and, like a soldier wounded on the battlefield, carried Sweetboy's metaphorical stretcher to a metaphorical Huey chopper so that our Lord and our God could fly him to safer ground even as Agent-Orange Evil was hovering over his face like a cloud.

THE JOY COMES IN

SWEETBOY WOKE UP ON July 3rd. I remember this because I had recently finished a novel I'd been working on in which a prayer vigil is held on July 3rd for a comatose girl. I found that remarkable. That night Rick and I went home together for the first time. A nurse promised to call if there was anything at all they thought we'd want to know.

Later that same night I got a call from the nurse. She told me Sweetboy had wanted her to call me. "He wants me to tell you he's sorry and that he loves you," she said. I stared at the open door with light flooding in from the hallway bathroom. I asked her to please tell him I love him too, tell him I love him so much. I thought about going across to the hospital, then rolled over on my side and quietly cried.

* * *

Rick and I were sitting next to Sweetboy's bed when a doctor I didn't know showed up. She didn't say hello but went straight to the curtains and briskly pulled them open. His breathing had been labored to the point of him asking me about it and I didn't know what to tell him since I'd been concerned about it too. I could see his chest rising and falling and his speech was labored. Nurses weren't checking on him as much as they had been at first and it made me nervous, I felt that if anything serious happened, it would be up to me to call someone in. After she opened the curtains, I asked her why his breathing was so labored.

"That's what drugs do to you," she said and left as quickly as she'd come in. I still don't know if she meant the antibiotics or the heroin. I think she left it for us to figure out.

After that, a social worker came and talked with him. She told him if he was healthy enough he would be discharged to a rehab in a few days. When she left, Sweetboy sat up and peeled off the tabs and the wires stuck to his chest that were monitoring his heart, pulled out his IV, and left the hospital. He was about to leave still wearing a hospital gown when one of the nurses gave him his jeans. We begged him to stay but he left anyway. I wanted to struggle him to the floor, tie him to the bed, anything to keep his warm body where I could still touch it. Heartbroken, Rick and I went home. I tried to get the peace that I had in the elevator and think about how no matter what everything would be okay. I was a little bit successful.

When we got home, we found him in his room with his head in his hands. He looked at us and told us he couldn't do it, that he couldn't go to rehab and if we made him, he'd only leave. We said he had to and that he didn't have a choice. We had found a rehab that was supposed to be a very good one. It was beyond our ability to pay for, but at that point it didn't matter. We could sell the house if we had to. We told him it was only an hour away, *Get your things together, we're going.* He said, "I can't," and to underscore that we were going anyway, I grabbed a bag from his closet and put a few things in it I thought he would need. Rick led him out to the car. Sweetboy was sweating and pale and shaking. I wondered how many beats per minute his heart was beating and if it would suddenly stop and if there was a defibrillator at the rehab.

Sweetboy got in the front seat next to Rick and I got in the back. Rick's dad had come down by that time and he came out the back door and headed toward the car. He was about to get in the back seat with me when I told Rick that I didn't want him to come with us and that I thought we should be alone. Rick seemed reticent at first, but when his dad slid in next to me, he told him it would be best if he stayed here. "Oh, okay," he said, and slid back out.

I tried to keep my tears to myself as we quietly pulled out of the driveway and onto the highway. Rick appeared calm. We were silent. Sweetboy rolled his window half down and lit a cigarette. I stopped crying as we passed farms and fields planted with knee-high corn and soybeans. It was gray out and every once and a while we'd pass one of the many newly redesigned rest stops. Halfway there my brother called. He said he wanted to pay for rehab.

When I heard his voice, I started crying again. "It's so much money."

He was reassuring and calm, I could tell he wanted me to know it didn't matter how much it was. "How about I start by sending $15,000?"

"I can't believe how much it is. I'm so sorry. Thank you so much. I can't believe you're doing this. Thank you, thank you so much." I spoke quietly. I didn't want Sweetboy to hear me.

Wyomissing, Pennsylvania, although it sounds similar to Wyoming, is nothing like Wyoming. Wyoming is dusty and waterless, like an expanse of cracked, dry skin. Wyomissing is lush and green. It thrives. Narrow roads wander through trees so intertwined some of the trunks have become grafted together into fat pasta-like contortions. There are pockets of houses and antique shops, oil paintings, chairs, things made out of tin placed on sidewalks to lure the occasional bevy from the city. Farm tables and pottery. We headed up a mountain to the rehab center. The road wandered between tall pines in wide switch-backs. We passed a few cleared areas with cabins and outdoor fire-places and they made me hopeful, as though all we were doing was dropping Sweetboy off for summer camp where he would canoe and swim and learn archery and meet a cute girl. I began to imagine rehab solving everything; it would all be over soon. We'd have him back, and I would no longer be afraid.

I prayed in a series of paragraphs, each one slightly different, but in all of them asking God to heal our son. Between each paragraph I caught my spiritual breath, thanked God for something, and continued on. The rehab was situated in a wide clearing at the very top of the mountain. There was a large sign like you might find for a new housing development named *Forest Knoll*, or *Meadow Fields*, as though com-bining two pastoral words together will automatically fill the place with laughing children who will never think of doing drugs. *Village Greens, Abington Ridge, Orchard Ponds*, all of them fake like Kensington is fake.

As we pulled in, I immediately hated the place. Although there was an enormous old farmhouse and another older mansion, and the place was clean and well kept, there were no cozy cabins or archery targets or canoes, some of the buildings had faux stone siding and the windows had plastic inserts as stand-ins for real mullions and for some reason I just plain wanted everything to be real. We parked in a lot next to a small building with a sign that said "Admissions." I grabbed Sweetboy's bag and we got out of the car. There was a round white pergola next to the parking lot with a stone pathway that led to the building. Each stone was engraved with a step from the twelve-step program: admitting you have a problem, higher power, yadda yadda yadda.

Inside there were two small glass windows, one with a sign taped to it that said *Please take a seat, someone will be with you shortly.* There was a comfortable hotel lobby–like couch and two hotel lobby–like yellow chairs and an oval coffee table. A box of Kleenex. Good call. Behind the couch was a large, fading photograph of what looked to be the facility in the fall. The carpet was the type you might find in CVS, nondescript gray with virtually no give. You could bounce a basketball on it. The room had an affliction of blandness, as though every drink of alcohol or needle of dope rejected—every day *without*—had the anemic side effect of no longer being able to experience color, and the photograph of the facility in the fall with its faded reds and yellows and greens had been hung there like a prescription drug to mask the side effects of detoxing. Rick went over to a Keurig coffeemaker and made himself a cup of coffee. Sweetboy looked out the window. He was still shaky and sweating. His face was pale. I looked for a defibrillator.

A kind woman came around the corner, introduced herself, and shook Sweetboy's hand. We followed her to a small room with a conference table and comfortable chairs and sat down at one end. Protocol. Questions. Sheets of papers to fill out. A male nurse came in and took Sweetboy to a room around the corner to make sure he was physically okay and part of me hoped he wasn't okay, that he'd be sent back home with us and I could squeeze myself backwards through some kind of hole in the spacetime continuum and build a fort with him in the backyard.

Is all of this odd? Am I more distraught than other parents who've been through the same things? If Sweetboy was angry and fighting us would I have been less distraught? Or more distraught? I don't know the answer to this.

When Sweetboy's counselor came in to meet us, we immediately liked him. He was warm and understanding and confident, like he understood how difficult things were for us. He told us that Sweetboy was in the right place and would be okay. I don't remember his name, only that he made me feel hopeful. He said he'd be in touch to let us know how things were going. His office was lined with books, books on addiction, Bibles, concordances, C. S. Lewis. He told us later that Sweetboy had spent a lot of time in there hanging out and reading.

* * *

When we got home Sophie and one of my friends were cleaning up the kitchen and sweeping the floors. My friend was sweeping dog hair off the stairs and asked me whether there was always so much dog hair and how can you keep up with it. Usually I would have made a joke about it, mentioned something about how we should shave Joey once a month or something, but I just smiled and gave a half-hearted laugh and said I know. There was a bag full of food on the dining room table, a salad, and chicken and rice, and I could smell it as soon as we came in. I wasn't hungry but the thought of someone caring for us by bringing food almost startled me. As though like a prism, there were facets to what we were going through that we hadn't begun to see yet. Smells are memorably strong. Sometimes God being good to me can make me uncomfortable the way receiving from others can make me uncomfortable—it's hard to think I deserve it.

By that time it was late at night and Sophie suggested we should rest so we went to the guest room and lay down, prayed quietly, and fell sleep. Three hours later I got a phone call from Sweetboy's counselor.

"He ran about an hour ago and since he isn't eighteen yet, we can still go after him, but I sent some staff to find him and they weren't able to. I'm not sure why he left—things seemed to be going well. Everyone seems to like him here. His roommate is kind of upset. I've actually had to work to calm him down some. I thought I should let you know right away—this kind of thing happens a lot."

Wyomissing is near Reading. If he made it to Reading he'd find heroin. If he did heroin, his heart would fail. If his heart failed, he would die. We got in the car and we headed back to look for him somewhere within the forty-mile radius encircling Reading. Somehow we'd find him. At least if he hadn't caught a bus to Oregon.

Like a manual I have to keep flipping through to find the right page, peace eludes me when I'm looking for it. Biblical hope is really the opposite of hoping; biblical hope is the sense of expectation arising from a fact understood by faith, and when we were driving through city streets and up winding mountain roads desperately looking for Sweetboy, I was *hoping* we'd find him, but what I really wanted was to *expect* we would find him. I wanted to be confident that the outcome would be victorious even though confidence that it would be, in effect, was impossible unless I *believed* the ending would be victorious. (And I don't mean manipulative belief, the way some might say, "*If you only believe* such and such will happen," as though it's a matter of mustering up something in ourselves to make a specific thing happen.) Of course, we don't know what that victory will look like, only that it's a good thing, and if it's a good thing, there's peace in that. Some of the root words for faith are *assurance* and *firm conviction*. Belief. Faith. Trust. A spaghetti of words. In philosophy it's called a conditional. I needed hope after all, I just didn't understand what the word meant.

Christian Wiman wrote his poem "From a Window" after being diagnosed with cancer. The poem touches on how perceptions can change when experiencing grief and suffering. In the last stanza he writes, *That life is not the life of men / And that is where the joy came in.* God transcends the life of men, and as I wound up a hill in Reading, Pennsylvania, looking for Sweetboy, I finally found that page in the manual I'd been looking for. A lot of conditionals, but things began to come together.

* * *

We found him walking down a hill not far from the rehab, and when he got in the car he gave me a small yellow flower. I pressed it flat between two fingers and held it tight for the rest of the day. The Sweetboy I knew would give me a flower—Sweetboy, who weighed ten pounds nine ounces when he was born and when he was four stood on the chair in the kitchen to help me bake cookies, would give me a flower.

After we picked him up and began to drive back up the mountain so that he realized we were taking him back to the rehab, he said he wouldn't stay. He was becoming agitated and Rick talked to him the whole way up, explaining how important it was, that everything would be okay, and I prayed. I prayed that he'd go in and stay. I prayed rehab would change him. I prayed that he'd never do drugs again, but when we pulled into the parking lot he jumped out and ran toward some woods and disappeared. It was very dark. The last thing I saw was one leg, the bottom of a sneaker, and his middle finger; and then he was gone.

Worse than needles and intubation and comas and septic shock will always be that finger in the air; it was the antithesis of the flower he gave me and it symbolized much more than the finger itself did. It symbolized one of two roads he could take. The flower symbolized the other. First the flower, then the finger, and I had no idea which one would win. Is it possible to hand someone a flower and at the same time flip them the bird? Would that cancel both of them out? Insert irony so that the whole altruistic/blasphematic act is obliterated?

Rick and I drove home. When I finally got into bed, Rick was already snoring. He'd been so levelheaded. I was wide awake and I knew I wouldn't be able to sleep. Not knowing where Sweetboy was was the colossus of my emotions. It shouldered its way past everything else and made sleep impossible; eating too.

I lay there listening to Rick snoring. Before Sophie's wedding there hadn't been any curtains on the windows, so I'd made some in haste out of some burlap I'd found in the basement and you could see right through them. It was a corner room; one window faced the backyard, which was dark, and the other faced the neighbor's driveway and garage, which had a light above it. The light came into our room as though sifted through gauze, hitting the bedside table then touching the floor before it disappeared.

The phone rang. Some number.

It was Sweetboy.

"Hey, can you come get me?" He was mumbling.

"Where are you? Tell me where you are."

"I don't know."

"We'll pick you up, just tell me where you are."

"I'm at some restaurant. I don't know, it's near a town." He began to sound irritated.

"We have to know more—Sweetboy, is there anything else? What's the restaurant called?"

"I'm not sure, it's a little farther down the road from that parking lot next to the hill."

"Stay there. Whose phone are you using? Don't go anywhere."

* * *

We drove back and forth on the road for twenty minutes before we found him. He was at a restaurant, *Wyomissing Restaurant and Bakery*, on the left, after a firehouse. When we pulled up he was waiting next to the parking lot with an older guy. When we got out, Sweetboy introduced us to him, "Hey, this is Mike."

We shook hands and told him thanks for letting Sweetboy use his phone. It was a short conversation. He told us he'd picked him up walking on the side of the road and that he looked so young he thought maybe he needed help so he took him to the restaurant and bought him a meal. We said, "Thanks so much, thanks, thank you." Sweetboy said, "I really appreciate it"; the man said, "Of course," and headed to his car.

We got a room at a hotel and decided we'd think about what to do in the morning. Sweetboy told us the guy at the restaurant was really nice and had been clean five years, that he'd shown him a gold coin he'd earned from AA, and I thought maybe angels are like that, maybe sometimes they don't wear brilliant white shirts but look just like people so they won't scare you.

The next morning we talked. I didn't know what to do, I had no idea what to do. I knew if we took him back to rehab he would run again and it would accomplish nothing, perhaps even make things worse if he made it to Reading. Mostly I prayed. Rick took him outside and they talked for a long time. I was glad to be alone.

In the end we decided to take him home. He agreed to go to another rehab, only an outpatient one, and be tested every day. We drove home. He rolled down the window and lit up a cigarette.

* ✳ *

The humbling that parents experience when a child is lost in drugs is a precious thing. That invisible seed of humility (that, when pullulated becomes authentic love, selflessness, compassion; tools bound, albeit invisible, to a parent from the first day their baby sees light) needs to make its striking—its beautiful—appearance. The humility of everything falling apart, of every loved thing you have veering away like a meteor slipping from orbit, reveals your true state of affairs.

And something else wonderful happens when you stop obsessing about how you're perceived. In 2 Corinthians 1, the only passage of the Bible I've ever memorized, it says we comfort other people with the same comfort we've received from God. If I wasn't willing to be honest about what we were going through, I doubt many people would have opened up to me about their own struggles; I wouldn't be much use to any unfortunate kindred spirits out there. You can't comfort someone with a wayward child if they think your own kid studies hard, gets up early to walk the dog, and makes you breakfast every morning. So I think in the end humility—that same thing we're always running from—makes rubble of The Evil. It's all about being humble because when you're humble you start to pray and when you pray you're comforted and when you're comforted you comfort others.

WAYS TO SAVE A KID

THERE ARE TWO TYPICAL WAYS to deal with alcohol when it comes to kids. One theory goes like this: if you don't freak out about alcohol, if you demonstrate to your child that it can be enjoyed in moderation, it will remove the novelty of it, and thus take away any desire they might have to go get blotto when they're older. Ultimately, they'll be less likely to abuse it. The likelihood of rebellion is diminished since there's nothing to rebel against. A child taking a few sips of wine from an adult's glass becomes an inoculation.

The other view sees twenty-one as the only acceptable age for a sip of anything, other than cough syrup, that has alcohol in it. A sip of wine before age twenty-one is not okay. Self-control, respect, rule-following, prevention. It's a parent's duty to make sure their child is following the rules, and that includes not drinking alcohol before it's legally permitted.

Until recently, within reason, I would probably have leaned toward the first view. Rick and I don't drink much, so it wasn't something we gave much thought to, but it makes sense to me to allow a sip of wine here and there. A sip of wine at fourteen to see what it tastes like doesn't seem harmful, maybe even beneficial. No big deal. Teach them moderation, all's good.

Richard Mattick and his colleagues at the University of New South Wales in Australia monitored the alcohol intake of almost two thousand teenagers, age twelve to eighteen, over the course of six years ("Association of Parental Supply of Alcohol with Adolescent Drinking, Alcohol-Related Harms, and Alcohol Use Disorder Symptoms: A Prospective Cohort Study," *The Lancet*, January 25, 2018). They specifically focused on the parent's role regarding whether or not they allowed their child to drink in moderation at home, even if it was only a sip of wine here and there. They were looking for correlations related to future binge drinking.

The results surprised me. While it wasn't a clear one-to-one, overall the kids who were supplied alcohol at home were more likely—at 81 percent—to self-report binge drinking as they grew older. Teens with no access to alcohol reported having the least amount of alcohol-related problems.

However, keep in mind that this study was based on self-reporting, which provides for a good measure of unreliability, and doesn't take into account whether a child was given a case of Carleton Draught or a couple sips of Merlot. (Also, some European countries with lower drinking ages have been assessed as being the "least risky" for later drinking problems in young people by the World Health Organization.) Stuff to think about.

As it turned out, Sweetboy had a very addictive personality and I don't think either strategy would have necessarily prevented anything. Familial genes are peculiar things. One child wrinkles his nose when Aunt Phyllis gives him a sip of her Pinot Noir, another one asks for a second. And for some people, marijuana is poison. If you inherited a variation of the AKT1 gene, a bong hit or half-inch roach can be enough to trigger psychosis: depression, mania, schizophrenia.

If, with genetic testing, we could discern the likelihood that someone will develop an addiction later in life, would it be possible to prevent alcoholism the same way you prevent anaphylactic shock from a stray peanut? Could we prevent addiction to oxycodone or cocaine or heroin or meth? Could parents clasp a silver bracelet with a red caduceus to their child's wrist as a warning, to warn people they aren't like other kids—that their child is hereditarily predisposed to addiction and should not be given certain substances *ever*? Could that same parent drill these things into their child from a young age so they'll know that if they ever abuse drugs—even one pill or hit of weed—for them it will lead to rehab, jail, or death? I like the idea of a bracelet with a caduceus on it. Prevention is always better than treatment.

I recently read an article in *The Atlantic* by Gabrielle Glaser ("The Irrationality of Alcoholics Anonymous," April 2015) that postulates that the success of Alcoholics Anonymous—as well as rehab—is significantly lower than certain prescribed drugs in preventing relapse. (The article focuses mainly on alcohol addiction, although much of it is apropos regarding opiates as well.) In short, both alcohol and opiates bind to receptors in the brain that produce dopamine, the neurotransmitter responsible for producing a feeling of well-being, then tickles them into overdrive so they experience a super-duper feeling of well-being rather than your basic, *What a beautiful day, perhaps I'll take the dog for a walk and then invite my good friend Sally over* sense of well-being. Certain drugs, such as Naltrexone, bind to these same receptors and elbow out Mr. Alcohol or Mr. Opiate so that you can get back to enjoying a beautiful sunny day in the way that beautiful sunny days are meant to be enjoyed; in short, the drug prevents an addict from getting high.

Just like cancer, ways to save a kid are about prevention and treatment. There's the nature and the nurture and the studies and the medicine and rehabs, and for a parent it can feel like standing in the middle of a rotating circular platform trying to figure out what to focus on. It was disconcerting to bring Sweetboy home from rehab. We wanted so much to do things right. We tested him. We took him to IOP. I sold his car and hid the keys to ours. I kept nothing but a dribble of gas in it so that if he ever did get the keys, he wouldn't make it to the city. It caused the fuel pump to go, but it was well worth it for the peace of mind it gave me.

GOLDEN BOY

FOUR WEEKS AFTER we brought him home I still wanted to chain Sweetboy to his bed so he couldn't go to the city. Before I sold it, I unscrewed a spark plug from his car like a nun from *The Sound of Music*—I took advantage of any opportunity for control, and would have bricked in his windows and slid slices of pizza under his door for dinner if Rick would have let me, but Sweetboy did seem to be doing well. We faithfully tested him every day. It takes a month for weed to leave the system, so we were eager for him to test negative for it. One afternoon, Rick stood outside the bathroom and waited for his sample:

"What's taking so long?" Rick said. It had been a few minutes, and still Sweetboy was in there.

"I can't go."

I yelled from the living room, "We'll wait!"

"I'm shy."

I was starting to worry. I looked at Rick. "He's shy?"

"It's a thing. Guys can't pee when people are looking. Or waiting."

"What about if you're at a urinal?"

"Right, it's a thing."

He came out and handed me his T-cup. I felt the sides to make sure it was warm and took it upstairs to wait for the results. Sometimes I tested Stephan too. He was always clear.

It was clean. One month after his overdose, Sweetboy tested completely clean. Blue staccato lines up the side of a plastic cup. Not one drug in his body. I placed the cup on the mantel like a trophy.

* * *

There are always the horrible stories about prison, and even though I'm sure there were many stories to tell, the only thing I heard about Waylen when he was in prison was that he sang in the church choir. Stephan told us this and it made Rick laugh. I pictured him standing on the upper row of a set of bleachers because he's so tall, or maybe in the middle, singing "How Great Thou Art" and "I Have Decided to Follow Jesus," but I'm sure that's not the way it was. More than likely they sang the Christian songs you hear on the radio. Maybe they rapped in the choir; maybe there were a few gifted prisoners that stepped down off the risers and belted it out.

In prison they make everyone buzz their hair. It was hard to imagine Waylen without his hair, I wondered if I'd even recognize him. If he wasn't wearing his ponytail, his hair was striking: honey gold and soft curls. He was tall, but in my mind he was still a boy. The most lost of The Lost Boys. His ponytails and smile and homemade bows and arrows in the backyard. His shorts in the basement after he left. Stephan said when he had to cut his hair in prison he actually liked it, without the blond curls bleached by the sun, his hair was dark, just like everyone else's. He looked like a man's man. Of course, once he got out of prison he let it grow out again.

I'm not sure how long it was before he used heroin again, only that a month later he still wanted to stay clean. I didn't see much of him, but he and Rick got together a few times and almost every night Stephan stayed at his place to keep him from going out and talked him down when he needed to be talked down.

One night Stephan asked us if Waylen could stay here for a while—it would be safe and he'd have Rick to talk to and he'd feel like he was a part of a family. I knew it could be the difference between him going back to his old friends or staying sober, but I also knew by then that sobriety can be short lived and that it's easy to be fooled, that it's not always obvious when someone's doing heroin and sometimes you don't know they're shooting up again until after they're making trips to The Badlands once a week and it's too late to turn back now.

You know how sometimes people say things like I *love* so-and-so, only the real reason they're saying it is to hide the fact that they hate so-and-so? That it might as well be followed by *however*—that in fact so-and-so irritates them to no end? There was no *however* when it came to Waylen; we just loved him. We loved his long hair and his smile and his aviator sunglasses, and we loved that morning when he and Rick prayed together and Rick told him he would be dead in a few years if he didn't stop using heroin. Waylen didn't irritate us to no end, we plain loved him, and even as I write this my eyes are starting to tear up. I loved him but I said no, I love you Waylen, but you can't live here.

I texted him after that and told him I was sorry, *I wish I could say yes but I can't, I'll only worry. About you and about Sweetboy.* I was so tired. I was sleeping too much. All I wanted to do was sleep. *I love you and I'm really sorry but I know it's the right thing to do.* He texted back:

"I understand its ok"

I texted back, "I really want you to stay here"

"I know and I totally understand"

I texted, "I'm so sorry"

"its ok you know I'd never do anything though right? not with sweetboy"

"I know Waylen I believe that. I love you"

"love you too"

Later on he bought flowers for me. Stephan put them upstairs in my studio so I could look at them when I worked.

* * *

Sweetboy had been sleeping in the downstairs guest room, and one day he asked if he could move back up to his old bedroom across from ours, the one with the crawlspace and the eaves and the slant of sun in the afternoon. He and I spent the rest of the day taking apart his bed and hauling up clothes. Before we moved the furniture in, and when he was about to put his rug down, I told him to wait so I could clean the floor.

While I was down on my knees with a rag and a bucket of soap I remembered a confusing verse in the Bible that talks about scrubbing your house after an evil spirit leaves, and to be careful because after it's all clean seven more evil spirits could come in. On my knees with the wet rag, I told Sweetboy what I could remember about the verse. "I know, I know," he said.

*　✳　*

I began lining up the clean pee tests on the mantel as a joke. Sometimes I made them into pyramids. Humor helped me feel like things were wrapping up; I'd stamped Sweetboy's overdose as *that was then* and begun to get up earlier and eat and do the necessary things required to get to a healthy old age. The T-cups on the mantel became my art. I would stack them and line them up and arrange them in all manner of patterns. I even humored myself by thinking how easy it would be to turn the whole mantel-T-cup thing into performance art; pouring pee from cup to cup, tossing something at them, stacking one on top of the other like Jenga blocks and watching them fall. I thought all of this was very funny.

Week after week and then month after month he tested clean. Sober, sober, sober, sober, sober, six months sober, seven months sober . . . eventually I stopped testing as much. Occasionally I would, but not often.

THE REVELATIONS
OF DOORS

HOUSES ARE DEFINED BY THEIR DOORS. Like the way a hairstyle can hint at someone's personality, doors, if unhinged from their frames and removed to a faraway field, could tell legions about the house they came from; whether it was old or new or a colonial or ranch or split level or quaint or utilitarian or had a garden or nothing but overgrown conifers, whether it was full or empty or warm or cold. Houses with solid wood doors hint at prelapsarian youths spent playing in rose gardens, while hollow doors imply Saturday morning cartoons and tuna fish casseroles.

The most defining characteristic of a door is whether it's a hollow door or a solid door. I grew up in a house built in the 1970s that had second-generation hollow doors, which are better than first-generation hollow doors only in that they have secret locks. The only way to lock my childhood bedroom door was to press the knob in and turn it slightly to the left, but it could easily be opened from the outside by inserting a paperclip into a small hole in the middle of the knob. There was a tiny lever, or tab, and if you pressed it the knob would turn and the door would open. It was an exciting thing to discover at eight years old, the hidden lever that opened locked doors.

The house we live in now is a collection of both solid and hollow doors with a few present-day fabricated ones thrown in, so that none of them, lying in a field somewhere, would reveal that the house was built in 1953. Our hollow doors have no locks to speak of, and some have indentations where a foot or elbow, something, banged into it—it doesn't take much more than a slight smack of an elbow to make a dent. A few of them have actual holes. You could drop a penny in them and punch another hole at the bottom to get it out. These kinds of doors are easy to kick in.

Sweetboy, to make a little money, had begun doing mailings for Rick. Often, when I came downstairs, he would be at the dining room table surrounded by papers and stamps, folding letters and tucking them into envelopes. One afternoon I noticed he looked pale, but also flushed, as though underneath the pallor of his face there was a red flush riding up his neck and inching over his cheeks. There was a kind of grayness and he looked like he'd been sweating. I asked if he was feeling okay.

"Yeah, I'm fine."

"Really? Because you look like you're sick."

"I'm okay." He kept folding letters then got up and went outside for a smoke.

Later that same week, around ten in the morning, Rick and I were in the living room working on our computers. Things were good. Like the apostle Paul, I had begun to pray without ceasing, thanking God. Everything was going to be okay. Sweetboy would finish college and get a job and get married. We would have grandkids and take them to the lake to swim.

My computer was about to die so I went upstairs to get the cord. When I passed Sweetboy's room, I knocked lightly on his door to wake him up. He'd always had a hard time getting up so I often had to knock on his door numerous times to get his attention. I went back downstairs to work. Half an hour later he still wasn't up so I went upstairs and knocked again, harder this time. Twenty minutes later he still hadn't come downstairs up so I went up again, banged on the door, and yelled. That's when Rick ran upstairs and kicked the door in.

Sweetboy was propped up against his headboard with his computer sliding off his lap, one ear bud in an ear, the other lying on his chest. His head was slumped over to the right and he was blue.

When we saw him, some kind of trebuchet fission split us and we both ran; Rick into his room and me out of it. I grabbed my phone, bent over shaking, moaned in such deep sorrow I wasn't sure it was my own voice, and called 911. Rick pulled Sweetboy off the bed, held him up against the wall, and slapped him over and over trying to wake him. He pounded on his chest and slapped him and yelled his name. Later, when we told a nurse that he had kept hitting him to try to wake him up, she said it's what she would have done. I don't know if Rick did CPR or not. I don't think I'll ever know, because even though Rick said I could interview him for this book, when I sat down in the kitchen with a notepad and asked him what happened after he kicked the door in, he said, "I . . . ," stopped short, looked at the floor, then said, "I'm sorry, I still can't talk about it."

I was hunched over in our bedroom trying to call 911 and Rick was trying to make our son breathe again. God had abandoned us.

* * *

Job's wife tells him to curse God because he's nowhere to be found. John the Baptist, waiting to have his head cut off, tells one of his disciples to go ask Jesus if he really is the Christ and when given the affirmative, hunkers down and waits for the sword.

If everything you thought was good is turning to crap, you have to wonder if it was really good to begin with. I felt like I was back in college curled up on a beanbag chair afraid of not believing in God.

* * *

The dispatcher was calm, which I assume they're trained to be, but it's a horrible thing, because when your kid is not breathing, you want them to be as upset as you are. You want them to care as much as you because then they'll call an ambulance faster, prep the ER, whatever has to be done. They have to be freaking out almost as much as you're freaking out or your boy won't live. *Please, he's not breathing, please, just come now!*

"Is he responsive?"

"No! He's blue, please get an ambulance here," and I told her my address, and again and again to hurry.

Calmly, "They're on their way."

I ran outside, stood on the lawn, and looked down the street. The dispatcher told me to stay on the phone. "Why aren't they coming? They should be here by now." I was still shaking. The front door was open and I could hear Rick still trying to wake him up. The ambulance didn't come and it didn't come. "They should be here by now!"

"It's only been"—she was so freaking calm—"three minutes."

"We live across the street. We live two blocks from the hospital . . ."

"They'll be there shortly." Truly, she sounded bored. She was probably eating lunch.

When they finally arrived they pulled forward and took the time to back in the driveway, the ambulance slowly beeping until it came to a stop. What the hell? I told them he was upstairs, "the door on the right, *please hurry, please just hurry . . ."*

They headed into the house. One of them asked if anyone was with him.

"Yes, my husband, he's trying to revive him . . ." *Run! What are you doing!*

I followed them closely up the stairs as though I was planning on shoving them into the room, then stood in the hall, at which point they began to work fast, ripping open medical paraphernalia: needles, gauze, paper, and dropping them on the carpet. Things landed on his chest, a needle on the floor. They brought up a stretcher, lifted him onto it, and slowly inched back downstairs.

As they were headed down, Sweetboy's eyes fluttered open for a moment and he mumbled, "Am I going to die?" before drifting off again. I stood on the lawn as they slid him into the ambulance. Rick and I got in the car to follow them to the hospital and Rick hugged me. "It's okay," he said, "I'll believe for you."

The same emergency room doors. This time we followed him into the ER and watched as they attached the IVs and tabs for the heart monitor. They clamped a pulse monitor on his finger and covered him with a light blanket. His eyes fluttered open then closed. I asked a nurse if he was in septic shock. She told me he had some sepsis. Stephan came and sat on the floor. I cried. I asked if he was going to make it. Sweetboy opened his eyes and groggily asked again if he was going to die. The nurses wouldn't answer him. Rick told him he would be fine and that everything would be okay. He said it a few times and I said, "Don't say that." Rick, angry, took me into the hall and asked why. I told him to stop lying because we still didn't know whether he was going to make it. Rick said he wanted to encourage him. I told Rick if Sweetboy makes it through this, I want him to know he almost didn't.

I think about the second overdose as one of those memories that are the opposite of nostalgia. Nostalgia hits the senses like a water that runs fast and clear, where you can see things like crawdads and pebbles and minnows the size of fingernails swimming in clusters under the surface. Bad memories come at you like a kind of destabilized molecular disassociation because as hard as you try to make them, they won't ever form a pattern.

TRIPPING

EVEN THOUGH THE doctor in the ER said the heroin had been cut with so much crushed up rot it was impossible to figure out what it was, Sweetboy was going to be okay. And to put a spiritual bow on a spiritual package, and to affirm that I do in fact still believe in God, I'll point out that if he never had this overdose he could have kept using. It was a sovereign overdose. Opiates, like smoking, weigh as heavy in the veins as they do the heart, and a body too familiar with them is a body that craves like a baby craves its mother.

Although plenty of people wax on about how we should live life to its fullest, like it's one long beautiful ribbon—*live, love, laugh,* ad infinitum—it's also a life of sorrows. But there can be contentment in both. Not contentment with the sorrow, but contentment in spite of the sorrow. If we metabolize sorrow with even an iota of wisdom it's possible—like drinking fresh water from streams lit with plankton— to experience the peace of an amaranthine God. This is what St. Paul says in the Bible. I might be an inattentive Christian but I depend on an attentive God.

* * *

They moved him upstairs and sometimes Stephan or Christopher would visit. We joked and talked, happy because of the pure fact that Sweetboy was still with us. This time, if he went through withdrawals at all, they weren't severe since he hadn't been using long—as I understand it, he'd gone to the city with Spider-Kid, bought three bags of heroin, and overdosed on the first bag. I asked him where the other two were and when he told me I went home to get rid of them.

It was around 10:00 p.m. and Rick had gone home to rest; he was exhausted. He'd prayed all night for Sweetboy the night before and slept little. When I got home he was lying on the bed praying again, so I slipped into Sweetboy's room to get the heroin. I'd never seen it before: the tiny—almost translucent—glassine pockets, the miniscule paper lunch bags protecting less than half a teaspoon of fragile powder loose in the creases. Forgetting that Stephan had dropped bags of heroin in Rick's lap—that Rick already knew well and good what heroin looked like—I thought I should show it to him. I went to our room and sat down on the bed. I opened my palm so he could see it.

"Want to see what it looks like?"

He looked at it and didn't say anything.

"I've never seen it before," I said. "I hate it."

He reached out and touched it.

I found some scissors, went to the bathroom, cut it into little bits, flushed them, and went back to the hospital.

Forty minutes later I was at the hospital again with Sweetboy. It was after 11:00 p.m. by that time, and we were discussing when he could come home. Sometime while we were talking Rick came in and quietly sat down in a chair on the other side of the bed. The halls were empty of nurses and the room was dim, lit only by a small fluorescent light above Sweetboy's bed that had a long string he could reach to turn it on and off. Rick sat silently with his elbows on his knees and looked into the middle distance. I made a useless joke about hospital effects—the dinner tray still there since five o'clock with the ugly green plastic cloche covering some cold, unknown food, the plastic mugs and plastic pitchers—and slowly poured lukewarm water from a pink carafe into a brown mug. I handed it to Rick, then placed a flimsy pink vomit basin on Sweetboy's lap. "Just in case," I said. He smiled.

I looked toward the hallway, "No one's been in for a while."

Sweetboy fingered his IV. "I don't really need this anymore."

"Yeah, well you gotta keep it in," I said. "You need the vitamins, the nutrients. It prevents scurvy." I was still joking about everything, as though the whole event was one last necessary skim off the top of his life before he would settle back into the real Sweetboy—that same ten-pound, nine-ounce baby who grew into the loyal kid who made rockets and boats out of cardboard—and as long as I remained lighthearted nothing would change that.

Rick pulled his chair closer to the bed and took a deep breath. "Something just happened."

I looked at him. He still wasn't looking at us. "What do you mean?"

"I can't explain it. I'm not sure. I don't know, everything came alive, like the dining room chairs. They were like cartoons, only evil—but they didn't scare me. Everything had a personality. Everything was evil but I wasn't afraid. And bright, like extremely vivid."

"Wait, what?"

Sweetboy was staring at him.

"It was some kind of paranormal experience."

"You dropped acid," Sweetboy said, "you had to have."

"No, it started as soon as I touched the heroin. Everything got really vivid."

"You had to of taken something," Sweetboy said. "Are you sure you didn't? By accident? You had to of."

"Wait," I said. "What? I'm really confused."

"No, I didn't even take a Tylenol," Rick said. "It started right when I touched the heroin. Right when I touched it an audible voice said, 'Lazy motherfucker,' and then everything immediately changed."

"You were tripping," Sweetboy said. "You had to of been," and he started asking Rick questions. "Did everything come alive? Like trees?"

"Exactly. Everything was personified, like they had little smiley faces on them and they were terrifying, only I wasn't afraid."

"Did you feel like you were connected to them?"

"Yes!"

And the two of them started talking, sharing experiences, Sweetboy asking clarifying questions and Rick answering in the affirmative. It was startling. They were experiencing some kind of new connection that I didn't understand. I just listened. Sweetboy was telling Rick what it felt like to do LSD and Rick kept nodding.

"You were definitely tripping."

"It was so strange."

I asked Rick, "Do you still see things? Is everything normal now?"

"Yes, it started when I touched the heroin and stopped when I got to the hospital."

"You were definitely tripping," Sweetboy said.

* ✳ *

I don't know if Timothy Leary ever stayed in our house in 1967 and left psilocybin decomposing in the rafters, but something triggered what Rick experienced that night. Rick didn't take anything, but by that time little surprised us. By then The Lost Boys had dragged in enough supernatural gimcrack that what happened could almost be expected. From what I understand, acid trips are confusing as much as they are revelatory—like heavy-lidded contorted truths—but then truth isn't truth if it's in bed with a lie. Regardless, I'm not the one who had the acid trip so this is all speculation.

We doubled down again. By then, minus fresh pee falling from the bathroom ceiling, cheating on a test was impossible. The only way to pass a test if he had drugs in his system would have been to replace dirty pee with clean pee, and I made sure that didn't happen. There would be no stranger's pee strapped to a leg, no powdered pee in a pocket or synthetic pee in a plastic cup waiting in the shower stall. I didn't rest until I knew of every possible way to cheat and eliminated them. But the truth is, Sweetboy wanted to stay clean.

His countenance began to change. He got a job and went back to school. Rick would stand outside the bathroom door and wait—T-cup after T-cup, week after week became month after month became a year became a year and a half became two years. This time, when I tested him, I didn't bother making art on the mantel. I threw the cups in the trash until I didn't have to anymore because I stopped buying them to begin with.

I had a dream that tiny seed pods, like boys, were bursting in the air like cottony fireworks and each time one burst, more seeds sprouted out and floated up into the wind until there were millions of them, tiny seeds scattering and bursting. Every time one exploded it was remarkable and more than I could handle it was so beautiful, but then another would explode. I'd think it was all over but then another one would burst and scatter its seeds. It was like each pod was a boy holding the love of a multitude and I was watching as they all took flight.

KAYAKING THE
DARK RIVER

At one point Sweetboy tried to quit cigarettes, and of course we were thrilled. I assumed it would mean a week of irritableness and then he'd pull out of it, squeaky clean and smelling of Ivory soap, but I swear, there should be someplace with rubber rooms and nothing but air holes for people to detox from cigarettes, because without cigarettes, Sweetboy was immediately inhabited by a squirm that nearly popped all his blood vessels.

One night in early fall, void of nicotine and particularly kvetched, he asked Rick to drop him off with his kayak at the Brandywine River then pick him up farther downstream, which Rick was happy to do, as being outside tended to clear Sweetboy's head. It was a dark night and there wasn't a moon. Rick helped him struggle the kayak on top of the car, and as they pulled out of the driveway I could hear them talking. It was such a pretty fall night.

Rick dropped him off at a small park with a picnic table and two parking spaces right next to the river where it bends to the left then disappears behind a thicket of bushes and poison oak climbing a large dead tree. When he got home Rick told me that after he backed the car up to the river and helped Sweetboy get the kayak into the water, it was so dark he could barely see his shadow as he paddled around the bend and disappeared into the darkness. I asked him if Sweetboy had his phone and he said yes.

Half an hour later he called Rick and asked him to pick him up at another park downstream but when Rick got there he couldn't find him—it was hard to see anything—so he went to the middle of a stone bridge to see if he was approaching from upstream. The river was shallow and running slow. Without rain the usually mud-spongy grass at the river's edge is firm, with no muck to sink into, and rocks appear like shark fins in the barely moving current. When Sweetboy finally called him, Rick told him he was standing on the bridge looking, but he couldn't see him or hear him. In the stillness, and without the usual sound of fast running water, Rick thought it would be possible to hear the faint echo of the kayak, of paddles dipping into water or hitting the hollow plastic of the boat. Sweetboy tried to explain where he was but it was so dark he couldn't see anything; every tree was the next tree and the water was without rhythm or color. There was no marker or house or fence to direct Rick to. He didn't know how far away from the bridge he was, or if he was even close to it.

They hung up and Rick held his phone above his head like a beacon while Sweetboy kept paddling, pushing himself through the shallow water. At one point it was too shallow to float and he climbed out of the kayak and dragged it down the river as it scraped the riverbed. Rick kept his phone in the air until he began to hear the scraping and

bonking of paddles on the boat. He yelled and Sweetboy yelled back—
he yelled that he could see the light and Rick watched as his son, slowly
and arduously, made it to the bridge.

When they got home I asked how it went and Sweetboy said it was
so dark it was kind of terrifying because he couldn't tell where he was.

WALKING IT BACK

I'VE OFTEN WONDERED that if $E=mc^2$ were to allow it, and I could
head back down that mountain in Wyomissing to find that he'd
never experimented with drugs or snorted a pill or shot heroin; had
never left youth group or went to the Brandywine to smoke weed—
if that first cigarette had never entered his mouth; if he'd kept his
boyhood friends and went to camp and learned to build fires and
pack light for hikes into the mountains; if he'd eaten his vegetables,
and hadn't thought twice about the vitamins plus iron in the medicine cabinet; if he'd weighed eight pounds nine ounces, not
ten pounds nine ounces when he was born, would heroin have
bothered with him? Would The Evil have never left its banks and
violently sideswiped Sweetboy?

This is a mind game I shouldn't play, but it's a tempting game for a
parent. When you're going through the various tumults that accompany having a child caught in addiction, control steps up like a
potential hero, but shrivels in the end. When we mess around with "if
onlys" and "what ifs," oddly and irrationally, we're trying to stamp our
present knowledge onto our past ignorance, as though what we know
now can retroactively heal all things. Like that song by The Faces, "Ooh

La La," we reggae next to our dark oceans—*I wish that, I knew what I know now / When I was younger . . .*

But you didn't know then. If you're E=mc^2-ing, you're accomplishing nothing. As the apostle Paul says in Philippians 3:13-14, "But one thing I do: forgetting what lies behind and straining forward to what lies ahead, I press on toward the goal for the prize of the upward call of God in Christ Jesus."

That peace I experienced in the elevator as we ascended to the CCU came with a sudden revelation that caused my "what if?" to become "even if." Of all of the mind games a parent—or anyone who loves an addict—can play, "what if" is the worst of them. We roll the dice but we don't want the ones and there's always a moment where the breath holds still before the dice land. That moment of air is the most painful thing because what if we roll snake eyes? We can try not to think about them, but it's still possible to roll them.

My peace came when I realized that snake eyes or no, everything would be okay. As counterintuitive as it might seem to someone who's not a Christian, I realized that even if I lost my son and experienced the unimaginable pain I knew it would bring, my God is a good God and a loving God and someday, as it says in the book of Revelation, he will wipe away every tear from my eyes.

* ✳ *

I prayed often that Sweetboy would grow into a wise and praying man. Four things happened that I took as promises from God that Sweetboy would thrive. They were random things, and odd, but for some reason I was moved by each of them. They gave me an assurance that things had changed forever, as though every crumpled can and plastic bag and cigarette butt within Sweetboy's radius had been swept into a massive pile and burned.

One time he and I were driving through town and the traffic slowed so that we came to a stop next to a kid on a bench nodding off. We were both looking at him when Sweetboy told me his name. "That's so sad," I said, and we pulled away. Nodding off on a bench was a distant life for him that was only growing fainter.

Another time when I was in town by myself I saw an old man— perhaps in his late seventies. His yellowed teeth were barely distinguishable from his rotting gums and the edges were worn down and dark, like they'd been brushed with black chalk. I imagined him smiling wide, like the whole point of him smiling was so I could examine his teeth. I smiled at him as he passed by.

One day I went for a run in a park where I often prayed and I stepped on a snake. I didn't see it until it was under me, and then it glided away like a fish in water, back into the grass. A few days later I went for another run and stepped on it again, but this time it was dead.

A month or so later we went with some friends to a state park where we climbed up a steep path to picnic under two enormous shade trees. Their trunks were so thick the bark had separated and split in long, dark crevices. From the hill you could see rolling fields planted with corn and soybeans. Our friends had a newborn baby and I held him so they could eat. They'd given the baby his father's name, which is also Sweetboy's name. He'd been born on Sweetboy's birthday and his hair was the same auburn color that Sweetboy's had been as a baby. As I held him I walked farther up the grassy hill and stood next to a field of corn. I looked at the expansive valley dotted with trees and fields spread so far I could see our town in the distance. As I held him I sang a song; I don't remember what. I have a terrible voice, but the baby didn't mind.

WAYLEN

ONE AFTERNOON I came in the back door with a bag of groceries. Before I put it on the counter Rick walked in. There was something sad about his eyes, and when I asked what was wrong all he said was, "Waylen." We hugged and cried for a long time.

Stephan was sitting on the front porch, staring at nothing. I sat down next to him and hugged him tight because it was all I could think to do.

SUNFLOWERS

IT'S BEEN A LONG TIME since Sweetboy's second overdose and Rick's mystifying, unexplainable acid trip. The Evil hijacks brains and bodies for a good laugh if nothing else; its invisible Uzi with its forked tongue that spits into crowds and fells whoever it hits. The Badlands are a sagging net of half-alive people, and as one fifty-three-year-old addict recently said, "A lot of people die down here, and they're letting them die because they don't want the cops to come, so they push the bodies to the side."

The Evil's spit grazed Sweetboy's head and heart and they bled something awful, but it in the end it wasn't a direct hit because both overdoses, although they came very close to killing him, stopped him short. I prayed and God yanked him aside before anything lodged in his skull. The scars are there, at least for me, but they're tough with faith and I don't think there's a needle on the face of the earth that could penetrate them now.

Last spring I went for a walk. It was a beautiful day so I decided to walk up an alley and look at the gardens behind the houses. There were fences covered in roses and blooming clematis and the grass was that dark green—that unparalleled beauty that can hurt it's so beautiful to look at. There were a few wooden gates and some of them were open. I could see the back doors of the old houses with vines climbing above them and smell the sweet honeysuckle that I remember pulling the pistils out of as a child and sucking out the nectar. As I walked up a short hill I noticed three kids walking toward me—two boys and a girl—around thirteen or fourteen years old, and they were laughing. One of the boys yanked something from a vine and threw it at the girl. She ducked and then punched him in the shoulder. As I passed them I smiled and was going to say hi but they barely noticed me. I stopped when I reached the top of the hill, turned around, and prayed they would never do drugs.

Sweetboy has a dog now, a black lab that he got from the SPCA with a short tail, and when the dog sees Sweetboy and excitedly wags his tail, its length makes it look like it's wagging double-time, faster than the tails of other happy dogs. His love for Sweetboy is manifest in that tail, as though the dog is wagging grace, as though every swipe in the air is erasing every needle that touched Sweetboy's skin.

Last year Sweetboy took the dog with him on a camping trip, strapped on a small backpack made for dogs, and put his food in it for him to carry. The hike was difficult, uphill and with a lot of stones, and when he got back two of the dog's paws had cuts on them, so he cleaned them and bandaged them and began looking online for padded dog shoes so it wouldn't happen again. Another time he and Jeremiah hiked to a river and set up camp on a small patch of land that jutted out into the water. That night they heard a pack of wolves growling like they were right outside the tents circling a carcass. Jeremiah stood outside next to the tents with his knife ready to stab anything that came close and Sweetboy stayed in the tent to protect his dog that was curled up and shaking next to him.

That winter Sweetboy bought a row house in town and planted sunflowers in the backyard that grew a full foot taller than me. He brought me three of them and I put them in a vase above the fireplace until their powdery yellow dust began to fall in a golden shadow on the mantel. Sunflowers blow my mind the way their faces stare at the sun all day, turning as it passes from east to west. They remind me of stars in awe of the light, stars like the faces of children, mesmerized by the warmth of a generous sun.

A long time ago, when I wanted to be like Suzanna Wesley with my head draped and a cup of tea on the table, I didn't know that ten of her children died. She had nineteen children and nine of her children died as infants. Four of the children who died were twins. One of them died when a maid accidentally smothered her. When Susanna herself died, only eight of her children were living. Her husband, Samuel, left for a year because of a minor dispute and then spent time in jail because of financial issues. Also, their house burned down twice.

Susanna didn't see any of those nine children come back to life, and God didn't save them from death even though I imagine she prayed herself crazy that they wouldn't die. I've discovered that when that murmur of angst begins doing its thing—which it can still do—turning my body parts to wax, it helps to remind myself of that platitude that no one else is allowed to say to me and *trust God*.

PROVENCE

We were in France because my brother was turning fifty. I like to say my brother has a charmed life. And I'm not even sure if it's his down to earth, beautiful wife or the vineyard or the trips or his three beautiful children. I think his charmed life has less to do with those things and more to do with generosity. He and his wife live palms up and they flew us to France where we stayed in a villa in Provence that overlooked vineyards that retreated into the valley below and then rose up on the other side to the town of Venasque, its ancient buildings clustered on top of the mountain as though carved from rock. Our first morning there I woke to the distant sound of the church belfry, its deep ring vibrating and then thinning as it spread into the air.

The last day we were there we hiked to Venasque. It took us less than forty-five minutes, and instead of taking the narrow switchback road that leads to the village we hiked a trail straight to the top; it was a steep path covered with stones and roots, and more than once I had to stop and catch my breath. There were cherry trees and sycamores with trunks that look dappled with sun and shade until you get closer and feel their papery-smooth bark that looks like camouflage from far away. You don't feel deceived when you find out the tree is different up close; it feels more like you've discovered the tree's true beauty, the smooth outside that hints at an undiscovered depth within.

The story of Abraham willing to sacrifice his son Isaac is in the twenty-second chapter of Genesis. Abraham was old and didn't have a son but God had promised him one so he trusted God and kept waiting. He was still waiting when he turned one hundred and his ninety-year-old wife, Sarah, conceived. When the baby was born they named him Isaac.

There's something about a son. There's something about a daughter too. But there's something about a son. When I sat with Sweetboy on my lap in the emergency room after he drank the cough syrup or when he ate the bottle of vitamins plus iron, I felt overwhelmed by the son thing. Maybe it was because of the emergency room, some vague feeling that I could have lost him, or maybe it was the sheer amount of time that we sat there, his head leaning back on my chest as I stroked his soft auburn hair from his damp forehead. Maybe it was because he's my only son, the only son I have, as though I was beginning to realize he would one day move on and I only had so much time left with him. I think for girls it's different. I think they need you for life and you stay close forever. I think we hold our sons tightly because they're only with us for so long.

And so when God tells Abraham to take his son, *his only son*, and sacrifice him on Mount Moriah—literally lay him on an altar, raise his knife and kill him—that son thing must have struck his own heart, as though the knife he carried was already lodged in his own gut and with every step up the mountain it wiggled around mashing his organs to bits.

Abraham bound his son, his only son, and went up to a mountain.

We're allowed access to almost everything: Abraham gives Isaac the wood to carry, and takes the fire and the knife, and leads his son up the mountain. And then this: "And Isaac said to his father Abraham, 'My father!' And he said, 'Here I am, my son.' He said, 'Behold, the fire and the wood, but where is the lamb for a burnt offering?' Abraham said, 'God will provide for himself the lamb for a burnt offering, my son.' So they went both of them together."

But here's the thing: even though he commands Abraham to do this, God seems more sorrowful and heartbroken than Abraham does. Each time he refers to Abraham's son, he doesn't stop at "your son," he goes on to say, "your *only* son." "Take your son, your *only* son." It's like God is mourning his lost son more than Abraham is, like he's mourning the loss of *his* only son, Jesus, who he knows will one day be crucified.

When we reached the top of the hill at Venasque, the path turned to stone stairs. We rested there, and when I looked up at the belfry, I saw—like a scene from a movie—a flock of pigeons fly out from it and scatter above the village. To the right I saw another section of stairs that led to a flat rock farther up the mountain. I started to climb.

The earth is so many live things pointing up: trees, blades of grass, even flies stalling on roadkill. There are the fires sparking into the night. There are humans. We're both obvious and obscure, I think. Our mere existence points to God and yet we hide like Eve behind a bush. We either fear his power or we don't believe in him because we can't have both, and without the magnificent thing I saw when I reached the top of that rock in Venasque, I would feel as insignificant as that fly on roadkill that doesn't have a clue where it comes from.

When I stepped onto the rock, sweaty and out of breath, I was met by a cool breeze and an expansive view of the valley below. The vineyards made a patchwork out of the land, the rows of tangled vines like threaded stitches, and I could see the villa where we were staying in the distance, but even as my hair parted with the first gust of cool air, I knew there was a crucifix beside me.

It was carved from white stone and the loincloth was painted gold. The paint was dull and chipping and was smudged onto part of one of his thighs as though it had been applied haphazardly. His head hung down to the left. His eyes were closed. The crown of thorns. The pierced side. The nails. The feet. His bleeding hands. The land spread out before him, the faraway grapes like so many drops of wine. He towered above me, and as the blinding sun reflected off the rock, I knew that I should remember what I saw, a scene like a vision to hold close for the rest of my life. This crucifix beside me. My majestic Christ who stayed put on the cross even though he owned the world.

In Genesis 22, when Abraham raises the knife over his son, a ram appears from the woods as a sacrifice in place of Isaac; Isaac is saved; and his father is saved from heartache unimaginable, because this is the way God works; and this is the way he loves; and this is the reason we trust him.

When we dropped off Sweetboy at the top of the mountain and he disappeared into the woods, Jesus had been standing on that mountain forever, his head hanging sorrowful, waiting for Sweetboy to finally look up. Jesus stays put for everyone even though he owns the world. He stays put for mothers in crack houses and babies full of opiates quitting cold turkey and screaming in pain. He cries for everyone, Jesus does. The meth addict on the street with the crazy eyes and the father who keeps leaving his family because he's following that fake love even though he's got the real thing right in front of him, the fifty-year-old with the tracks down his arm, his ankles, his neck. The girl, the boy, the kid, nodding off under a tarp-covered hut next to train tracks, the dealer hawking mollies on a dark street, the cheerleader snorting her mother's pain meds before school, the teenage boy who gives your teenage boy his first oxy to try because shit, that stuff is good. The man who rolls his unconscious friend out of the passenger side of his car at the doors of the emergency room because who knows, maybe he'll live after all. The leathery-faced blonde woman on the corner in her tiny jean skirt waiting for the right car and the right man and the right fix. The girl or boy or man or woman in their bedroom with a gun to their own head. The guy who gives his son his first shot of heroin. The boy in the pool house who won't wake up.

NOW

NEIL AND SOPHIE are in the kitchen cutting up sausages and vegetables for raclette. It's the holidays and there's snow outside and a cozy fire in the fireplace. Sophie has brought food and games for later and I can hear her and Neil joking about how she's a vegetarian but doesn't eat vegetables. I've turned the couch to face the fire for the winter and there's a leather sling chair to one side and an old yellow velvet wingback opposite it. Joey the dog and Sweetboy's lab eagerly sniff boots and crotches before they're pushed away.

I've lit five candles on the mantel and lined them up in a row beneath a late-nineteenth-century oil painting of dark ominous waves that I picked up in an antique shop in Lancaster. The fireplace is painted black and it makes the candles look even brighter. I hear Rick in the kitchen laughing about something and I think about how much I love his laugh and I think that it must make people feel known, that laugh. Someone is setting the table in the dining room and a fork or spoon hits the floor. Sweetboy stands behind his fiancée who's sitting in the leather sling chair and covering her chin with her turtleneck and laughing. He has his hands on her shoulders and leans down and says something. She slaps him lightly on his cheek and rolls her eyes.

Jules is home from San Francisco and is on her computer pulling up a video she did for work that I want to see. She pulls up another one she made on her own time and it's beautiful. It's about Black Lives Matter and it makes me cry. The back door opens and closes and I hear Jeremiah's voice and then Rick bursting into laughter and I know it's because he hasn't seen Jeremiah since he got back from a missions trip to India and he's so glad to see him. I smile when I hear them laughing. Stephan and Christopher come into the living room and sit down on the couch next to Jules. Jules is wearing a red sweater that says Budweiser on it, and black jeans and her hair is shoulder length and bleached blonde. She puts her feet on the coffee table and shows them her new shoes. She says something that makes them laugh.

We all go into the kitchen where Sophie and Neil have put out the food. Jeremiah digs into some hummus and Rick asks Stephan what he'll do after he gets his PhD. Christopher and Jeremiah, home from college, tell me about a professor they think might be homeless because sometimes he dries his clothes over the bushes on campus. They tell me how brilliant he is and that students love him. When we ask Christopher his plans, he says it turns out he's good with languages and wants to go into translations. We ask how Troy's doing, and Sam, and Quin, a boy who once brought his cello over and spent the night playing it in The Chill Spot, and he tells us Max has been hanging out with Manni, a kid Jules used to spend time with, and that Quin and Troy are working at a restaurant in town, but other than that he hasn't heard much. Sweetboy tells Rick how hard it's been to fix some wiring in the old house he bought, and Rick asks him if he's done with a complicated project at work; they talk about Java and Magento and Python and computer things I don't understand, and his fiancée tries to put a piece of broccoli in his mouth as he's talking. Rick asks him what he's doing tomorrow because we're all going to Longwood Gardens to see the fountains. Sweetboy's face looks beautiful to me and I know that I will always pray for that face, the healthy flush of his Irish cheeks and that magnificently strong heart that beats inside of him. I'll pray for his marriage and that he'll comprehend how deep and wide God's love for him is. I'll pray for angels to protect him and for any monsters to trip and smash their ugly faces to bloody bits if they even look his way. I'll pray for that one, sweet, pudgy baby, born years ago and lying in a hospital nursery like a half-grown king among a patchwork of normal sized infants; I'll go to him and pick up his fat hand and kiss it and bring him to my chest and shift my weight from one leg to the other—back and forth—and rock him and comfort him now, even before he needs comforting.

ACKNOWLEDGMENTS

WHILE I ALWAYS feel like I owe an apology to my early readers as they have to put up with all manner of redundancies and imprecise word choices. If it weren't for their willingness to read my first sloppy manuscripts and pass on their thoughts, this would never have made it to print. So much heartfelt thanks to Jennifer McNerney, Lyn Matejczyk, Mark Arnold, Avery Marks, Whitney James, Shane O'Neill, Amy Hanson, and Ellie Roth for your honest comments and suggestions. Please know that you made this book a better one.

To my editor, Ethan McCarthy, thank you for being smart. You knew what needed to go and what needed to stay and what needed to be rearranged all while you understood why and how I wrote this book to begin with. You are a gifted editor and I'm grateful for your hard work.

Ditto my copyeditor, Ashley Davila. Your tweaks and last-minute catches were indispensable. Thank you as well to Lori Neff, Allison Noble, and everyone at IVP who have helped get this book launched.

And finally, to all who have encouraged me and inspired me: Rick, our children, The Lost Boys, and everyone else who walked through our back door or up to The Chill Spot. I love you all dearly and I'll never forget our time together.